The CURVE of TIME

The CURVE of TIME

M. WYLIE BLANCHET

THE CLASSIC MEMOIR OF A WOMAN AND HER CHILDREN WHO
EXPLORED THE COASTAL WATERS OF THE PACIFIC NORTHWEST

SEAL PRESS

Published by arrangement with Whitecap Books, 1086 West 3rd St., North Vancouver B.C. V7P 3J6 Canada.

First published by William Blackwood & Sons Ltd. Edinburgh, 1961.

This Seal Press edition first published in 1993.

Cover design by Clare Conrad
Cover photo by Ron Watts/First Light

Library of Congress Cataloging-in-Publication Data

Blanchet, M. Wylie (Muriel Wylie), 1891–1961.
    The curve of time / M. Wylie Blanchet.
        p.   cm.
    Originally published: Edinburgh : William Blackwood
    & Sons, 1961.
    ISBN 1-878067-27-3
    1. British Columbia—Description and travel.   2. Boats
and boating—British Columbia.   3. Blanchet, M. Wylie
(Muriel Wylie), 1891 – 1961.   I. Title.
    F1087.B65   1993
    910'.9164'33—dc20   92-43650
                                                               CIP

Printed in Canada
10 9 8 7 6 5

Distributed to the trade by Publishers Group West

A view of Caprice

The author in the wheelhouse.

Capi

OOKING BACK NEARLY THIRTY YEARS IT IS HARD TO REMEMBER EXACTLY WHEN, BUT I think our first encounter was occasioned by a small car stopping at our front door. Out stepped a slight lady with brown short-cropped hair to welcome us as newcomers, identifying herself as the person living alone on the point at the end of the road.

She was matter-of-fact friendly, unassuming, with a no-nonsense side trying to hide a shy but rich sense of humour. Her name was Muriel Wylie Blanchet, but everyone called her "Capi." She was on her way to the village but just wanted to welcome us to the Curteis Point community.

It was an inauspicious start to a friendship, but my Eleanor and Capi soon found instant rapport, discovering a common interest in nature, art and literature. The drop-ins and exchanges continued, but neither one of us could have predicted that this remarkable woman, living at the end of the trail on seven waterfront acres with dreamy views of islands, mountains, restless boats and sea life, would turn our lives around.

In 1959 we had left the foothills of southern Alberta and arrived on Vancouver Island with four children who had to adjust from riding horses and a one-room country school to the ordeal of travelling by bus to a large institution full of strangers.

Curteis Point was a separate community of quiet achievers. We found ourselves surrounded by friendly neighbours in retirement from distinguished careers. On one side was R.M. Patterson, author of *The Dangerous River* and other titles published in New York and London. On his border was Captain J.D. Prentice who had commanded the corvette CHAMBLY, first RCN ship to sink a German submarine in the Second World War. Closer to us we were privileged to have Donald MacLaren, Canada's fourth-ranking First World War fighter ace, for another good neighbour. On the other side were the Pearces, retired from a career in Hollywood as make-up artists, and the Buckles, Tony and Prudence, whose children grew up with ours and kept lasting friendships.

Tony, ex-Indian Army, had been a contemporary of John Masters, adjutant of the Gurkhas, who had become internationally famous for his books on India.

It was a pretty heady environment after the isolation of a cattle ranch and they all made an impact on our lives. But no one more so than the shy, aloof, suprisingly competent and gifted Capi Blanchet who lived alone at the end of the road and involved us all in a quickly developing drama.

After six years of war and twelve grinding years in the foothills, we took time to adjust. That meant exchanging saddles for sail, so we acquired the 'Lady Mine,' a 24-foot sloop, and found a berth for her at Dick Johnson's wharf. Beside it was a 25-foot cruiser of modest mien, the 'Caprice,' soon to gain international recognition. Capi and her late husband had purchased it in 1923 for six hundred dollars.

When she came through the woods to check her boat, Capi would often find me banging away on a portable typewriter aboard our sloop. She had read my first book *We Found Peace*, published in 1953 by Thomas Allen in Toronto, about our struggles on the ranch and knew I was trying to write a sequel. Often, she would perch on the transom and read the pages I had just typed and we would talk about where I wanted to go from there. She never mentioned her own achievements with magazine articles and I don't recall her ever making any critical remarks except to urge me to keep at it.

By this time Eleanor and I were on a solid footing with Capi, and we will always remember the delightful times the three of us spent in the home she and her youngest son, David, had built after tearing down the old, original Maclure cottage.

Then one day she arrived unexpectedly with an urgent air and as much suppressed excitement as her poker-face would allow. She had just received a letter from Blackwood & Sons, Edinburgh, who had accepted her book *The Curve of Time* and were sending her a contract. Would we read it, and could we help her to understand what to expect? For the first time we realized that she had not only crafted articles for *Blackwoods Magazine* but also had sold pieces to several yachting magazines, and even had made it into the prestigious *Atlantic Monthly*.

We reacted to her news with joy and excitement. Just being

able to share the experience recalled our own giddy days when our story had been accepted. I may have been guilty of exaggerating what she might expect in the way of autograph parties, the hurdles of interviews by radio, critics and columnists. Carried away, I offered to act as her agent and help set up the publicity. Capi turned to Eleanor in dismay.

"He isn't serious, is he? If he is, you must stop him."

She managed to cool us down, and we all waited patiently for the lightning to strike, for the masses to discover this pleasing work, so lovingly written.

Nothing happened. During March 1961, Capi received six copies of the English edition, one for each child and one for herself. Eleanor was the first to read Capi's copy and was probably the first to realize that this work was a classic of coastal cruising, and something uniquely more. She had combined history and the environment as seen through the eyes of an artist who, in words, painted scenes and characters, mysticism and moods that were fast disappearing.

Capi wrote to Blackwoods for information and was told that seven hundred copies were being shipped to an associate in Toronto. Her friends in Victoria and Vancouver were anxiously impatient to read her book, and to help matters along, Capi made a loan to the small bookstore in Sidney so they could order copies from Toronto. The little book, 202 pages with a map and dust jacket in muted colours, sold for $3.25.

When she began to show signs of disappointment and frustration I went ahead and sent off reviews as far east as *The Beaver* magazine in Winnipeg. I managed to attract the attention of Bob Orchard, a CBC radio producer. He came to visit us, more than a little annoyed when he could not find a copy in Vancouver, and he managed to generate something.

Capi went back to her typewriter and stoically started to write a sequel, working in her bright and cheerful kitchen. She was typing away on September 30, 1961, when her heart stopped. They found her slumped over her typewriter with work in progress.

Don MacLaren came to tell us and we joined with her children for a private family service in St. Andrews Anglican church in Sidney. Our friend Canon Freddie Vaughan-Birch paid tribute to her life and her writing, holding a copy of *The Curve of Time*.

Then we all gathered at our Deep Cove home and were able to meet all her children. Six months was all Capi had to enjoy and share her creation, and she never knew the far-reaching importance her work would later come to enjoy.

The lesson was not lost on us. There must be a better way, we thought, for western authors to gain recognition. As we widened our circle of friends, fate seemed to point the way. Attending creative writing lectures at the new University of Victoria, I met a blind war veteran, Captain John Windsor, who at the age of 38 was trying to get established as a writer. We sent the completed manuscript to our friend in Toronto who said it was a good story but he could not see enough sales to justify publishing it. John tried another publisher in Toronto and received a cold rejection slip which left him dejected.

Obviously, there was a great need for someone in our region to start publishing, so we slipped into the slot, producing his first book, *Blind Date*.

As we gained confidence and experience the memory of Capi kept nagging at our conscience. The response to the small Black-woods' edition had brought a flood of appreciative letters from abroad to her children, with whom we had kept in touch though they lived in Golden, Vancouver and Victoria and one daughter in England. Finally we had a 'family conference' and decided to publish a Canadian edition. We added the material Capi had been working on when she died, and our editor stitched it all together.

The faith of her friends and family has been fully vindicated in successive editions. What a pity Capi cannot share it with us. Through all her disappointments I felt, somehow, that she knew she had created a legacy for all time. Nearly thirty years ago a critic in the venerable *Ottawa Journal* who had read the English edition, then discovered the first Canadian one, said "It's tempting to think that *The Curve of Time* will become a minor Canadian classic . . . striding tall as the B.C. coastal mountains themselves."

His musing has proven prophetic. Capi would have loved it. She had cast a literary pearl in the placid waters of Canadian literature to inform and please family and friends, and the ripples had spread, without a break, to the farthest shores. In the process she helped unknown writers, handicapped in many ways, to emerge.

To be invited to write this piece for a special edition to mark her book's thirtieth anniversary is a reward I never expected. My wish for Capi is that her classic may continue to be cherished by generation after generation of readers.

Gray Campbell

Editor's note:
This preface was written for a special Canadian anniversary edition of The Curve of Time. *Gray Campbell was the original Canadian publisher of the book and a close friend and neighbor of Muriel Wylie Blanchet.*

Hbr

QUEEN CHARLOTTE STRAIT

Knight
Inlet

Malcolm
I

Johnstone Strait

VANCOUVER

Pacific
Ocean

10 5 0   20   40

Scale in miles

The identities of Indian villages are
deliberately omitted at the request of
the author.

Foreword

HIS IS NEITHER A STORY NOR A LOG; IT IS JUST AN ACCOUNT OF MANY LONG SUNNY SUMMER MONTHS, during many years, when the children were young enough and old enough to take on camping holidays up the coast of British Columbia. Time did not exist; or if it did it did not matter, and perhaps it was not always sunny.

Our world then was both wide and narrow — wide in the immensity of sea and mountain; narrow in that the boat was very small, and we lived and camped, explored and swam in a little realm of our own making.

At times we longed for a larger boat; for each summer, as the children grew bigger, the boat seemed to grow smaller, and it became a problem how to fit everyone in. She was only twenty-five feet long, with a beam of six and a half feet, and until later, when the two oldest girls went East to school, she had to hold six human beings and sometimes a dog as well.

There were narrow bunks in the cockpit, butting into what we called the "back seat" which ran across the stern. Elizabeth slept in one, over the bedding and clothes locker. I slept in the other, over the gas tank and small food locker. We were quite comfortable. It was Peter, sleeping on the back seat over the big food locker, who complained when we slipped down too far in our bunks and got tangled up with either his head or his feet.

Up in the engine-room, which was separated from the cockpit by a solid bulkhead with a small door, there was a wedge-shaped bunk just for'ard of the engine. It started off with a width of four feet, but tapered to six inches in the peak. That was where the two smaller girls slept. There was no headroom in there — we had to crouch to get through the little door, and we had to crouch all the time we were in there — unless the hatch was open. But the children were quite comfortable, and with the hatch open at night they could lie there tracking down the different stars they knew, and gradually adding others.

That left John. John slept on a long pad down what he called the "crack," which was the eighteen-inch space between my bunk and Elizabeth's. In the early days no one could think what to do with John, until he solved the problem all by himself. We were busy one afternoon, cleaning up the boat, and nobody was paying any attention to what he was doing on shore. Once he came back to get the saw; then he spent the rest of the afternoon on the beach, very busy over something. Just before supper he climbed on board — the saw under one arm and a neat bundle of wood under the other.

"I'm not going to sleep down that old crack any more," he announced, as he spread out his bundle of wood and showed us. He had sawn up twelve twenty-two by three-inch boards and joined them all together with heavy fishing line, like a venetian blind. It fitted across the space between the two bunks, and under the two mattresses. The slats could not slip apart, for the line held them; yet it could be rolled up in the daytime and easily stowed away. The long narrow pad still fitted. He had anticipated all possible objections — there was nothing we could say. John had thought of a way to get himself up out of that crack, and was up to stay.

There was a two-by-two-foot steering seat just for'ard of Elizabeth's bunk, over a locker that held pots and pans and everyday stores. The gasoline stove fitted on top of the steering seat when in use, and folded up like a suitcase for stowing away. Its place was between the five-gallon demijohn of water and my bunk. Everything had to have its exact place, or no one could move.

We were very comfortable in the daytime with everything stowed away. The cockpit was covered, and had heavy canvas curtains that fastened down or could be rolled up. There was a folding table whose legs jammed tightly between the two bunks to steady it. And it was camping — not cruising. We washed our dishes (one plate, one mug each) over the side of the boat; there was a little rope ladder that could be hung over the stern, and we used that when we went swimming.

We may have grumbled about the accommodation; not about the boat herself. Lightly built (half-inch cedar) and well designed, she never hesitated to attempt anything we wanted her to try. She was uncomfortable in much of a beam sea, so for all our sakes we humoured her by working crab-fashion along the coast, first one way and then the other. But it was a following sea that she loved best; and after a long, tiring day it was never by her wish that we would give up and slip in to the sudden calm of a sheltered anchorage, where she had to lie, all quiet, and only gently stirring . . . .

Four of the stories in the book have appeared in *Blackwood's Magazine*.

M.W.B.
VANCOUVER ISLAND
BRITISH COLUMBIA

The Curve of Time

N BOARD OUR BOAT ONE SUMMER WE HAD A BOOK BY Maurice Maeterlinck called *The Fourth Dimension*, the fourth dimension being *Time* — which, according to Dunne, doesn't exist in itself, but is always relative to the person who has the idea of Time. Maeterlinck used a curve to illustrate Dunne's theory. Standing in the Present, on the highest point of the curve, you can look back and see the Past, or forward and see the Future, all in the same instant. Or, if you stand off to one side of this curve, as I am doing, your eye wanders from one to the other without any distinction.

In dreams, the mind wanders in and out of the Present, through the Past and the Future, unable to distinguish between what has not yet happened and what has already befallen. Maeterlinck said that if you kept track of your dreams, writing them down as soon as you woke, you would find that a certain number were of things that had already happened; others would be connected with the present; but a certain number would be about things that had not yet happened. This was supposed to prove that Time is just a dimension of Space, and that there is no difference between the two, except that our consciousness roves along this Curve of Time.

In my mind, I always think of that summer as the Maeterlinck summer — the year we wrote down our dreams. The children always called it — the Year of the Bears.

Towards the end of June, or it might have been July, we headed up Jervis Inlet. This inlet cuts through the Coast Range of British Columbia and extends by winding reaches in a northerly direction for about sixty miles. Originally perhaps a fault in the earth's crust, and later scoured out by a glacier, since retreated, it is roughly a mile wide, and completely hemmed in on all sides by stupendous mountains, rising from almost perpendicular shores to heights of from five to eight thousand feet. All the soundings on the chart are marked one hundred fathoms with the no-bottom mark . . . right up to the cliffs. Stunted pines struggle up some of the ravines, but their hold on life is short. Sooner or later, a winter storm or spring avalanche sweeps them out and away; and next summer there will be a new cascade in their place.

Once you get through Agamemnon Channel into the main inlet, you just have to keep going — there is no shelter, no place to anchor. In summer-time the wind blows up the inlet in the morning, down the inlet from five o'clock on. In winter, I am told, the wind blows down the inlet most of the time — so strong and with such heavy williwaws that no boat can make against it. I know that up at the head of the inlet most trappers' cabins are braced with heavy poles towards the north.

For some reason that I have forgotten, probably the hope of trout for supper, we decided to anchor in Vancouver Bay for lunch. Vancouver Bay is about half-way up Jervis, and only makes a very temporary anchorage good for a couple of hours on a perfectly calm day. It is a deep bay between very high mountains, with a valley and three trout-streams. You can drop your hook on a narrow mud bank, but under your stern it falls away to nothing.

After lunch I left the youngsters playing on the beach, and taking a light fishing line I worked my way back for perhaps half a mile. The underbrush was heavy and most uncomfortable on bare legs, and I had to make wide detours to avoid the devil's club. Then I had to force my way across to the stream, as my trail had been one of least resistance. It was a perfect trout-stream, the water running along swiftly on a stony bottom; but with deep pools beside the overhanging banks, cool shade under fallen tree-trunks. The sunshine drifted through the alders and flickered on the surface of the running water. Somewhere deeper in the forest the shy thrushes were calling their single, abrupt liquid note. Later, when the sun went down, the single note would change to the ascending triplets. Except for the thrushes, there was not a sound — all was still.

I didn't have a rod — you can't cast in this kind of growth, there is no room. I didn't use worms, I used an unripe huckleberry. An unripe huckleberry is about the size and colour of a salmon egg — and trout love salmon eggs. Almost at once I landed a fair-sized one on the mossy rocks. Another . . . and then another. I ran a stick through their gills and moved to another pool.

But suddenly I was seized with a kind of panic . . . . I simply had to get back to my children. I shouldn't be able to hear them from where I was, if they called. I listened desperately . . . . There was just no sense to this blind urge that I felt. Almost frantic, I fought my way back by the most direct route — through the salmonberry, salal, and patches of devil's club.

"Coming — coming!" I shouted. What was I going to rescue them from? I didn't know, but how desperately urgent it was!

I finally scrambled through to the beach — blood streaming down my legs, face scratched, hands torn — blood everywhere. Five wondering faces looked at me in horror. The two youngest burst into tears at the sight of this remnant of what had once been their Mummy.

"Are you all right?" I gasped — with a sudden seething mixture of anger and relief at finding them alive and unhurt.

After an interval, the three girls took my fish down to the sea to clean, the two little boys helping me wash off the blood as I sat with my feet in the stream. Devil's club spikes are very poisonous and I knew their scratches would give me trouble for days.

"There's a man along at the other end of the beach," volunteered Peter. "He's been watching us."

"All day!" broke in John. "And he's all dressed in black." I glanced up — a tall figure was standing there, against the trees, up behind the drift-logs at the top of the beach. Just standing there, arms hanging down, too far away to be seen plainly. Peculiar place for a clergyman to be, I thought inanely; and went back to the more important business of washing off the blood. Then I put on the shoes I had washed.

"Mummy!" called Elizabeth. I glanced up. The three of them were looking towards the other end of the beach.

"The man is coming over," said Fran. "He's . . . !"

"Mummy!" shrieked Jan. It didn't take us two minutes to drag the dinghy into the water, pile in, and push off. The man was coming — but he was coming on all fours.

The bear ate the fish that the children had dropped. Then, as we pulled up the anchor, not thirty feet away, she looked at us crossly, swung her nose in the air to get our scent, and grumbled back along the beach to meet her two cubs. They had suddenly appeared from behind the logs and were coming along the beach in short runs. Between runs they would sit down — not quite sure

3

what their mother was going to think about it. She didn't think it was a good idea at all. She cuffed them both, and they ran back whimpering to the logs. She followed, and then stood up again — tall, black, arms hanging loosely down, and idly watched us leave the bay.

"Mummy!" demanded the children, when they were quite sure they were safe. "That bad dream you had last night that woke us all up that you said you couldn't remember — was it about bears?"

"No . . . at least, I don't think so." But even as I spoke, I could remember how very urgent and terrifying something had been in that dream. I hesitated — and then I decided not to tell them about the strange, blind panic I had felt by the stream — I could have smelt the bear down-wind. But I knew that the panic and sense of urgency by the stream, and the feeling in my dream, had been one and the same.

Marlborough Heights flanks the northern side of Vancouver Bay, swinging boldly out in a ten-mile curve and making the inlet change its course. It rises straight up out of the sea, and straight up to six thousand feet. And nobody knows how deep it goes. The chart just states in chart language — one hundred fathoms, no bottom, right off the cliffs. The children always hang over the gunwale trying to see — they don't know quite what — but it must be something awful in anything so deep.

Peter and John were still moaning about the trout the bear had eaten — so I said I would stop and we would try to see what mysterious something we could catch. I stopped the engine, and Elizabeth held us off the cliff with the pike-pole, while we knotted all our fishing lines together. We tied on a two-pound jigger, which is a flat, rounded piece of lead, with a rigid hook at the lower end. Then we baited it with bacon, and down . . . down . . . down . . . and everybody watched and pushed for better places to see. After a while I thought I could feel something like bottom — it was so far away that I couldn't be sure. But I jigged the line up and down — up and down. Then something caught and held it and jigged back — somewhat like getting in touch with another planet.

I pulled in, and in, and in . . . . The children watched breathlessly, but still there was more to come. It was now definitely something. I told Jan to bring the dinghy in closer, and I leapt the gap, still pulling. I didn't know what might live at that great depth

— I'd bring it alongside the dinghy, have a look at it first and then decide.

Foot after foot . . . after foot . . . Then "Ah's!" from the children. A bright scarlet fish was goggling at me from beside the dinghy. It was about two feet long and thick through. It didn't struggle — it just lay there gasping. I took the gaff and lifted it gently into the boat by its gills, for water didn't seem to be its proper medium. Again it didn't struggle. It just lay on the floorboards and gasped and goggled as though it would have liked to tell me something, but couldn't.

"Put the poor thing back! Put it back!" pleaded the children, wringing their hands.

But just then, a great inflated tongue-like thing came out of its mouth and stayed out. Then I remembered what the fishermen up at the Yuculta Rapids had told us about the Red Snappers that were sometimes chased up from great depths. Without the pressure of the depths, this sack or bladder inflates, and they have to die. They can never go back to where they belong — and just flounder about on the surface until the eagles or seagulls put them out of their misery. They are very good to eat — but after seeing this one's goggling eyes and listening to its pleading gasps, I didn't think any of us would want to. I killed it quickly and put it over the side.

The wind hit us as we came opposite Britain River, just as it usually does. It blows out of the deep valley of the Britain River, and then escapes out through Vancouver Bay. After we had slopped ahead out of that, we met the wind that blows out of Deserted Bay and down the full length of Princess Royal Reach. So for the next ten miles or so we battled wind. It is not a nice wind in among the mountains. It picks you up in its teeth and shakes you. It hits you first on one side and then on the other. There is nowhere to go, you just have to take it. But finally, everybody tired and hungry, we rounded Patrick Point into the gentle Queen's Reach — and there, there was no wind at all.

An hour or so later we were at the entrance to little Princess Louisa Inlet. But the tide was still running a turbulent ten knots out of the narrow entrance — so we tied up to the cliff and ate our supper while we waited for slack water.

We were inextricably associated with Captain George Vancouver, R.N., in our summer-long trips up the coast. He explored, surveyed and charted the coast of British Columbia in 1792, and named practically every island, inlet and channel — names that are still used. Every bay we anchor in, every beach we land on — Vancouver or his lieutenants had been there first.

Vancouver of course had no charts — he was there to make them. But from old sources he had certain reports of a great inland sea in those latitudes — and he seemed to be convinced that it existed. Even when he was confronted with the whole stretch of the snow-capped Coast Range, he was still sure he was going to find a channel through the mountains to that mediterranean sea.

In June of that far-off summer of 1792, Vancouver left his ship, the *Discovery,* and the armed tender, *Chatham,* at anchor down in Birch Bay — just south of what is now the international boundary. Then, with Archibald Menzies, the botanist of the expedition, and perhaps four others in the little yawl, and Mr. Puget in charge of the launch, Vancouver set off to examine the coast to the north.

After exploring part of Burrard Inlet, on which the present city of Vancouver is built, they sailed up Howe Sound, just a little north of Burrard Inlet. Captain Vancouver clearly did not like our high mountains. The low fertile shores they had seen farther down the coast near Birch Bay, he says, "here no longer existed. Their place was now occupied by the base of a tremendous snowy barrier, thin wooded and rising abruptly from the sea to the clouds; from whose frigid summit the dissolving snow in foaming torrents rushed down the sides and chasms of its rugged surface, exhibiting altogether a sublime but gloomy spectacle which animated nature seemed to have deserted. Not a bird nor a living creature was to be seen, and the roaring of the falling cataracts in every direction precluded their being heard had any been in the neighbourhood."

Again — "At noon I considered that we had advanced some miles within the western boundaries of the snowy barrier, as some of its rugged mountains were now behind and to the south of us. This filled my mind with the pleasing hopes of finding our way to its eastern side." Then they proceeded up to the head of the inlet — "Where all our expectations vanished, in finding it to terminate in a round basin, encompassed on every side by the dreary country already described."

They sailed up the coast for about sixty miles, taking observations and soundings. Eventually, they entered Jervis Inlet. Starting off at four a.m. as usual — "The width of the channel still continuing, again flattered us with discovering a breach in the eastern range of snowy mountains, notwithstanding the disappointment we had met with in Howe Sound; and although since our arrival in the Gulf of Georgia, it had proved an impenetrable barrier to that inland navigation of which we had heard so much, and had sought with such sanguine hopes and ardent exertions hitherto in vain to discover."

Later — "By the progress we had this morning made, which comprehended about six leagues, we seemed to have penetrated considerably into this formidable obstacle, and as the more lofty mountains were now behind us and no very distant ones were seen beyond the valleys caused by the depressed parts of the snowy barrier in the northern quarters, we had great reason to believe we had passed this impediment to our wishes, and I was induced to hope we should find this inlet winding beyond the mountains."

After dinner they proceed . . . "Until about five in the evening, when all our hopes vanished, by finding it terminate, as others had, in swampy low land."

Vancouver's whole outlook on these beautiful inlets was coloured by this desire to find a seaway to the other side of the mountains. Some of the party must have been impressed with the beauty and grandeur. Menzies, the botanist, is more enthusiastic. In his diary he notes, "Immense cascades dashing down chasms against projecting rocks and cliffs with a furious wildness that beggars all description."

Even he doesn't say that the cascades start away up at four or five thousand feet. That mountains six and seven thousand feet high flank either side of the inlet beyond Marlborough Heights, and show great snowfields in the upper valleys.

Coming back from the head of the inlet that evening, Vancouver and his party, who had noticed the entrance to Princess Louisa on the way up and decided it was a creek, found the tide running swiftly out of it. The water was salt and the entrance shallow. They gave up the idea of spending the night there and rowed until eleven o'clock past high cliffs to find shelter behind Patrick Point.

7

The youngsters were delighted that Vancouver had missed Princess Louisa Inlet — very scornful that he had thought the entrance shallow.

"He didn't even try the right entrance, he was on the ledge," said Peter.

"Well, he couldn't have got in anyway, with the tide running out," said Jan, defending him.

He certainly couldn't have got in. Even we, who knew the way, were tied up to a log, eating our supper while the pent-up waters of Louisa poured themselves out through the narrow entrance in a ten-knot race.

It was also understandable that they should have mistaken it for a creek. From the outside where we waited, you can see nothing of the inlet beyond. Two steep four-thousand-foot mountains, one on each side of the entrance, completely obscure the inlet and the mountains beyond. The entrance is a little tricky to get through at low tide unless you know it, but there is plenty of water. From water level, the points on one side and the coves on the other fold into each other, hiding the narrow passage. It is not until you are rushed through the gap on a rising tide that the full surprise of the existence and beauty of this little hidden inlet suddenly bursts on you. It is always an effort to control the boat as you hold her on the high ridge of the straight run of water down the middle. Then, as you race past the last points, the ridge shatters into a turmoil of a dozen different currents and confusions. Your boat dashes towards the rocky cliff beyond the shallow cove on your right; and the cliff, equally delighted, or so it seems, rushes towards your boat. You wrestle with the wheel of your straining boat, and finally manage to drag the two apart . . . and you are out of danger in a backwater.

The inlet is about five miles long, a third of a mile wide, and the mountains that flank it on either side are over a mile high. From inside the entrance you can see right down to the far end where it takes the short L-turn to the left. At that distance you can see over the crest to where all the upper snowfields lie exposed, with their black peaks breaking through the snow. The scar of a landslide that runs diagonally for four thousand feet is plainly visible. At certain times of the day the whole inlet seems choked with mountains, and there is no apparent line between where the cliffs enter the sea and where the reflections begin.

Three miles farther down the inlet, the high snowfields become obscured — the mountains are closing in. You turn the corner of the great precipice that slightly overhangs — which they say the Indians used to scale with rocks tied to their backs: the one who reached the top first was the bravest of the brave, and was made the chief . . . .

Then suddenly, dramatically, in a couple of boat-lengths, the whole abrupt end of the inlet comes into sight — heavily wooded, green, but rising steeply. Your eye is caught first by a long white scar, up about two thousand feet, that slashes across . . . and disappears into the dark-green background. Again, another splash of white, but farther down. Now you can see that it has movement. It is moving down and down, in steep rapids. Disappearing . . . reappearing . . . and then in one magnificent leap plunging off the cliff and into the sea a hundred feet below. As your boat draws in closer, the roar and the mist come out to meet you.

We always tied up at Trapper's Rock — well over to the left of the falls, but not too close to the mile-high, perfectly vertical cliff. It is a huge piece about twelve by twelve with a slight incline.

"Did this fall off that cliff too?" somebody asked, as they took the bow-line and jumped off the boat onto Trapper's Rock. I was busy trying to drape a stern anchor over a great sloping rock that lay just under water, ten feet astern, and avoided answering. Dark night was coming on rapidly and the cliffs were closing in. Night was a foolish time to answer unanswerable questions. I was glad we couldn't hear the waterfall too loudly at Trapper's Rock. That waterfall can laugh and talk, sing and lull you to sleep. But it can also moan and sob, fill you with awful apprehensions of you don't know what — all depending on your mood . . . . My crew soon settled down to sleep. On the other side of the falls I could see a light through the trees. The Man from California, who had started building a large log-cabin last year, must be there — in residence. I didn't want to think about him, for he would spoil much of our freedom in Louisa . . . . Then I started feeling the pressure of the mile-high cliff, worrying about the two huge rocks we were moored between, and all the other monstrous rocks that filled the

9

narrow strip behind us. As you stepped off Trapper's Rock onto the shore, you stepped into a sort of cave formed by an enormous slanting rock that spread out over your head. A little stream of ice-cold spring water ran on one side, and dropped pool by pool among the maiden-hair ferns down to the stony shore. A circle of blackened stones marked our cooking fires of other summers. The back and top of this prehistoric cave were covered with moss and ferns and small huckleberry bushes. All the slope behind was filled with enormous rocks. They were not boulders, worn and rounded by the old glacier. They had sharp angles and straight-cut facets; in size, anywhere from ten by ten to twenty by twenty — hard, smooth granite, sometimes piled two or three deep — towering above us.

They were undoubtedly pieces that had fallen off the cliff, the cliff that shut off the world and pressed against me. The first night's question always was — was Trapper's Rock one of the first to break and fall, or was it one of the last, which fell and bounced over the others to where it now lay? In back of the rock, the masses are piled one on top of the other. There are deep crevices between them that you could fall into — no one knows how many feet. It would take rope-work to get on top of some of them. None of us is allowed to go in there alone.

The stars had filled up the long crack of sky above me. Brighter stars than you see anywhere else . . . bright . . . so bright . . . .

Somewhere in that uneasy night I dreamt that I was watching a small black animal on a snowfield, some distance away. I don't remember why I was so curious about it, but in my dreams it seemed most important for me to know what it was. Then I decided, and knew most certainly, that it was a black fox playing and sliding on the edge of the snowfield. Then moving closer to it, as you sometimes do in a dream's mysterious way, I saw that it wasn't a fox at all, but a small black pony. I remember that it looked more like a pony that a child had drawn — low-slung and with a blocky head — sliding on a most unlikely snowfield.

In the wonderful bright morning the cliffs were all sitting down again — well back. All the fears and tensions had gone. We had a swim in the lovely warm water. The sun wouldn't come over the mountain edge before ten, but a pot of hot porridge, toast and coffee kept everybody warm. I made the children laugh about my

10

dream of a black fox that turned into an ugly black pony. Everyone decided that it must have been the man in black down in Vancouver Bay that turned into a bear. I couldn't think why it hadn't occurred to me before. It's just as well to have dreams like that in the Past.

Over on the other side of the falls we could see a big float held out from the shore by two long poles — new since last year. Somewhere in behind lay the log cabin and the intruder. His coming last year had changed many things. We used to be able to stay in the inlet a couple of weeks without seeing another boat. Last summer, when the cabin was being built by skilled axe-men, there were always a few boats there — coming and going with supplies. And the men who were building the cabin were there all the time. We had only just met the Man from California, and we had stayed for only two days.

On the other side of the inlet, on the right-hand cliff beyond the falls, which is not as perpendicular and is sparsely wooded with small pines, there is a great long scar. You can see where it started as a rock-slide four thousand feet up. It had carried trees, scrub and loose stones in front of it — gradually getting wider as it scraped the rock clean. In rainy weather a torrent races down tumbling noisily from pool to pool. But in summertime only a thin stream slides over the smooth granite, collecting in an endless series of deep and shallow pools. Heated by the sun on the rock, the water is lukewarm. We used to climb up perhaps half a mile, and then slide down the slippery granite from pool to pool like so many otters. We found it too hard on the seats of our bathing suits, and had got into the habit of parking them at the bottom. Now, with the coming of the log cabin, we had to post a guard or else tie our bathing suits round our necks.

Boat scrubbed and tidied, sleeping bags out in the sun — everybody had their jobs. Then we collected our clothes for washing, piled into the dinghy and rowed across to the landslide. There was a green canoe turned over on the wharf; no sign of the owner. He probably didn't even know that anyone was in the inlet, for you can't hear a boat's engine on account of the falls.

The three lowest pools of the landslide were called Big Wash, Big Rinse, and Little Rinse. All snow-water, all lukewarm — so washing was easy. And we carry only one set of clothes, pyjamas,

11

and bathing suits — so there is practically nothing to wash anyway. We scrubbed our clothes — we washed our hair — we washed ourselves. That, interspersed with sliding, took some time. Then, all clean and shining bright, we gathered up our things. The three girls said that they would swim on ahead. Peter wanted to go too, but he swims with only his nose above water, and it is hard to see if he is there or not. So I said that he could help John and me gather huckleberries first.

When we followed later in the dinghy, Peter with his snorkel up, swimming beside us, there were the three girls sitting on the wharf, talking to the Man from California. He said he hadn't had anyone to talk to for a month — except old Casper down at the entrance, and he always brought back a flea when he went to visit him. He asked us to come over and have supper with him that night and see the new log cabin. The children held their breath . . . waiting for me to say — yes.

After lunch, needing to stretch our legs, we started off to scramble up through the mighty chaos that lay behind Trapper's Rock. Peter carried a coil of light rope for rescue work, and John his bow-and-arrow, ready for you can never tell what. We had to be pulled and pushed up some of the biggest barriers. Devil's club made impenetrable blocks around which we had to detour. Then suddenly we found ourselves on a well-defined trail that skirted all the biggest rocks and always seemed to find the best way.

"Who do you suppose this nice person was?" asked John.

"Trapper, I should think," I said, very thankful for it.

Then it ended in a big hole between two great rocks that overhung our way. The youngsters were intrigued with the thought of a real cave and wanted to explore it. But there was a very strong smell coming from it.

"Just like foxes," someone said. "No, like mink," said somebody else.

Certainly it was something, and we decided to skip it. We had to go partly through the entrance to get past . . . for some reason I could feel the hair standing up along my spine.

The trail led beyond as well. The huckleberries were ripe and the cave forgotten. Then we could hear the roar of the river ahead, so we left the trail and cut down towards the sea. We soon wished we hadn't, for the going was heavy and we were very vulnerable in bathing suits. Finally we broke through to the shore close to the falls; and there being no other way, we had to swim and wade back to our rock. I waded, with John sitting on my shoulders, up to my neck at times. The sun was off the rock, but the cliffs hold the heat so long that we didn't miss it. Later, each of us dressed up in his one set of clothes, we rowed leisurely across to the float, probably as glad to have someone to talk to as the Man from California.

The cabin was lovely. The whole thing, inside and out, was made of peeled cedar-logs — fifteen and twenty inches in diameter. There was one big room, about forty by twenty feet, with a great granite fireplace. A stairway led up to a balcony off which there were two bedrooms and a bathroom. A kitchen and another bedroom and bathroom led off the living-room. Doors, bookcases, everything was made of the peeled cedar-logs — even the chesterfield in front of the fireplace, and the big trestle table. A bookcase full of books . . . . A lot of thought and good taste, and superb axe-manship, had gone into the construction.

After supper, sitting in front of a blazing log fire, the children were telling him of our climb back into the beyond.

"And there was a cave, and it smelt of foxes," Peter burst out.

"Dead foxes," added John.

I asked if there were any foxes around here.

"What on earth made you think of foxes?" the man asked. "There are no foxes in country like this."

Then he asked questions as to just how far back we had been, and just where. Then he told us — a she-bear and her cub had been around all spring. One of the loggers who were building the cabin had followed her trail, and it crossed the river on a log some distance above the falls. He had found the den in the cave. Although he had a gun with him, he had not shot the mother on account of the cub.

Then, of course, the children had to tell about my dream of the fox that had turned out to be a black pony . . . shaped much more like a bear than a pony, I now realized. It all more or less fitted in. But what about the man down at Vancouver Bay who had turned out to be a bear? Maeterlinck was beginning to spoil our summer — if the dreams were going to work both ways we would soon be afraid to get off the boat.

The Man from California, who hardly knew us, was full of the

13

perils of the surrounding terrain. We were perfectly willing to say we wouldn't go near the bear's den again — we knew as well as he did that bears with cubs are dangerous. But we forbore to tell him that we were going to climb up four thousand feet the next day to get some black huckleberries we knew of at the edge of the tree-line. After all, *he* was the intruder — probably attracted the bears. Black bears like hanging around the edge of civilization. And this man and his log-cabin made the first thin wedge of civilization that had been driven into our favourite inlet.

Judging by the enormous stumps, at one time there had been a stand of huge cedars in the narrow steep valley. Just behind the new log cabin there is an old skid-road — small logs laid crossways to make a road to skid the big logs down to the sea, with a donkey-engine and cables. The skid-road goes up to about six hundred feet — back the way the old glacier had retreated. Cedar grows quickly, and in this moist valley, with heat and rotting ferns, the growth would be rapid.

Six hundred feet high doesn't mean that you get there by walking six hundred feet. It must have been two miles back to the little trapper's cabin at the end of the skid-road. The road slanted at quite an incline, and every muscle screamed with the punishment before we got there. We had to stop to get our breath every hundred feet or so — all except John and Peter who ran around in circles. At the cabin we dropped exhausted . . . then drank and bathed our faces in the ice-cold stream.

The skid-road ends there, and we had to follow a trapline marked by axe-blazes on the trees. The traplines are only used when the snow is on the ground, so there is no path to follow — just the blazed or white scars on the trees. We rested often, as the going was really hard — soft earth, moss and rolling stones. We had to walk sideways to get any kind of foothold. Then we came to the cliff. The boys thought it was the end of everything. But the blazes led off to the right, to the bottom of a chimney with small junipers for hand-holds. John went up directly in front of me. If he were going to slip, I would rather be at the beginning of it, before he gathered momentum. It had its disadvantages though; for he filled me up with earth and stones which trickled down inside my shirt and out my shorts.

At last — on the edge of a flat near the end of the tree-line — we reached the huckleberry bushes. Wonderful bushes! Waist high and loaded with berries twice the size of blackcurrants. Growing where they did, in the sun with the cliffs behind to hold the heat, and all the streams to water them — they are sweet and juicy. In no time we had our pails full — you just milked them off the bushes. And then we just sat and ate and ate and ate — and our tongues got bluer and bluer.

It was Peter who started sniffing, swinging his head in a semi-circle to pick up the direction . . . . "I smell foxes — no, I mean bears," he said. I had smelt them some time ago — bears like huckleberries too. But I hadn't climbed four thousand feet to be frightened by a bear. Also, I was getting tired of Maeterlinck conjuring up bears in our life. By now, everybody was sniffing.

"Bang your lids against your tins," I suggested. "That will frighten them away."

So we all banged and banged. Then, as our tins and ourselves were full, I eased everybody on down the trail — just in case. As was perfectly natural, everybody had dreamt of bears the night before. Well — Maeterlinck may have some kind of a plausible Time theory, but the children are not sure how he manages about the bears. If they are going to climb onto both ends of the Curve it will be a little too much.

Going down a mountain is easier on the wind, but much harder on the legs. The back muscles of your calves, which get stretched going up, seem to tie themselves in knots going down — trying to take up the slack.

We tried to sneak past the cabin to our dinghy at the float, but the Man from California was lying down there in the sun.

"Where have you been all day?" he asked. "I've been worried about you."

"We smelt bears," offered John. "And we banged our tins at them, and they were all as afraid as anything."

The man groaned . . . his paradise spoiled, I suppose. But what about ours? I hastily showed him the huckleberries and asked him to come over and eat huckleberry pie with us on Trapper's Rock — two hours after the sun went over the top.

Then we rowed home and fell into the sea to soak our aches and pains and mud away — around the rock, out of sight. We couldn't wear our bathing suits, for now our only clothes were dirty again, and we had to keep our bathing-suits for supper.

We made a big fire on top of the rock to sit by; and cooked our supper on the little campfire in the prehistoric cave. A big corned-beef hash with tomatoes and onions — our biggest pot full of huckleberry dumplings — and coffee. I had warned the children not to mention bears again, so beyond a few groans when he heard where we had got the berries, we had a pleasant evening.

Clothes had to be washed again — the mountain climb had certainly ravaged them. So we spent the morning away up the landslide while our clothes dried. The man had paddled off in his canoe early, to get mail and provisions that some boat was to leave for him at Casper's — so we had the inlet to ourselves.

I had snubbed everybody at breakfast-time who tried to report a bear-dream — and felt that I had things back on a sane basis again. I had dreamt of climbing all night — my legs were probably aching. It wouldn't do for me to write mine down when I had been snubbing the children for even talking about theirs. By breakfast-time the only thing I could remember about it at all — was hanging on to a bush for dear life, while something — water I think — flowed or slid past . . . . It had been terrifying, I know.

Later in the day we climbed up beside the falls. The stream above was very turbulent — you would certainly be battered to death on the big boulders if you fell in. And if you escaped that, there were the falls below to finish you off. Quite a long way farther back there was a large tree across the stream which made a bridge to the other side. We crawled across on our hands and knees — no fooling allowed. I brought up the rear, holding John's belt in my teeth . . . . The others were across and had gone on ahead before John and I got safely over . . . . I swear that either the tree or the shore shook with the force of that raging water.

The others were out of sight and I called to them to wait. When we caught up, we started to follow them over a steep slope of heavy moss. They were romping across, clutching onto the moss and completely ignoring the torrent sixty feet below at the bottom of the slope. Suddenly I was sure I felt the sheet of moss under my feet slip — as moss will on granite. I shouted to the children not to move, and worked my way up a crack of bare granite, pushing John ahead of me — then anchored myself to a bush. I

16

made the children crawl up, one by one, to where there were some bushes to hang onto. From there they worked up to a tree.

Elizabeth had to come to our help. Holding onto a firm bush, she lowered herself down until John could catch hold of her feet and pull himself up and past her. Then holding onto Elizabeth's feet, I put one foot on the moss and sprang forward, clutched a bush and then somebody's hand . . . . The youngsters were all safely anchored to a tree and I to a bush — and we sat there watching in horror as the big sheet of moss, to which I had just given the final push, gathered momentum and slid down and over the edge.

"I want to go home," wailed John.

"So do I," echoed Peter, his superior years forgotten.

"Don't be sillies!" I said sharply, recovering my breath.

"How . . . . ?" they all moaned.

"How what?" I snapped.

"Get home . . . . ?" they meekly sniffed.

Well, I wasn't quite sure at that stage. Besides, I was shaken. As soon as the moss slid, I had recognized the bush I was hanging on to — it was the bush in my dream.

Straight up seemed to be the only way we could go. Tree by tree all linked together, we finally got onto quite a wide ledge. And there on the ledge was a distinct trail.

"Why, it's that old she-bear's track again!" cried somebody.

"And that must have been her bridge!" said somebody else.

"Well, she certainly knows how to choose a good safe path," I said — wishing I knew which way she and her cub might come strolling.

I certainly didn't want to go over the trembling bridge again — so we followed the trail the other way. Going by the logger's tale, it should lead us to the old skid-road and then down to the cabin.

"Isn't she a nice old bear to make this nice path," said John hopefully — tightly clutching my hand.

"Silly!" said Peter, clutching onto my belt behind.

"Let's sing," I suggested.

So, all singing loudly, we followed the nice bear's trail . . . . A *nice* bear — whom I fervently hoped didn't care for singing.

Lakes

OMETIMES DURING THE LONG SUMMERS WE WOULD GET a longing to soak the salt out of ourselves. Charts are concerned only with the sea — they are not interested in what lies beyond the shores. They mark all the mountains for a mile inland — the highest ones with the altitude noted. But they are all aids to navigation. At the bottom of some charts they even have pictures of how the mountains rear and fold at the entrance to various sounds. Navigators approaching strange shores, and confronted with a solid line of mountains, know from the pictures that if they approach a mountain of a certain altitude, with other mountains that fold in a certain way on to either side — then a certain sound or harbour will open out as they approach closer.

But it has evidently never occurred to the cartographer that a small navigator might like to know of a small lake where he could soak the salt out. Archibald Menzies, the botanist who accompanied Captain Vancouver on the first trip up this coast, often made special notes of the waterfalls they came across. I expect they did use them for filling up the water casks as well. But I always have a mental picture of Captain Vancouver, Archibald Menzies, the botanist, and the other young gentlemen standing under the waterfalls — soaking out the salt.

After all, Vancouver's ships were on the coast for four months in 1792. They took shelter and anchored at night in the same coves as we did. They did most of their exploring in their small boats. Except for trying to make friends with the Indians, many of whom had not seen white men before, they lived the same kind of life that we did, and were concerned with the same kind of problems. So it is natural to suppose that they, too, liked to get the salt out at times.

Waterfalls are all right in their way, but they are usually cold. The lakes that over the years we have marked on our charts in red are warm. To qualify for the red mark there must also be a safe place to leave the boat. The lakes are often some distance inland, and you can't soak properly if you are worrying about your boat. It was sometimes fishermen, but usually loggers, who told us about these lakes. They would mark on the chart the bay in which to look for the stream — if we couldn't find or use the old skid-road.

"Just walk up the bed of the stream and you'll come to the lake. We were in there ten or fifteen years ago — logging," they would say.

Once, following directions like that, we were lucky to find the stream. If we hadn't noticed it coming out through the rocks at low tide it would have been impossible to find. There was an almost impenetrable fringe of alders, maples and salmon berries above the beach — which we worried and tore at. When we finally broke through, we were in a mysterious low tunnel of green growth — all clutching to hold us back. The little stream eddied and gurgled on its way to the sea.

It was twilight in there, and what with getting scratched with branches and slipping off the rocks, we one by one came to the conclusion that fifteen years was a long time to remember just which bay. At this rate we would never find the lake. Then, suddenly, it was lighter ahead, and the sun came through in shafts, making irregular, shimmering patches on the stream. At last we struggled and broke through onto the shore of the little hidden lake.

I don't know how long that little unnamed lake was — two miles at least, and perhaps half a mile wide. It was set down in the centre of pale-green growth — alders and maples that had rapidly covered the scars the loggers had left. And above the new growth more high, dark-green hills, fold on fold. Halfway down the lake a very disturbed loon was calling and calling . . . . I don't suppose anyone had been in here since the loggers had left, and probably its mother had told it that man never came here.

We swam and we soaked, then lay in the sun, thoroughly fagged out for the moment. Fresh water is enervating compared with salt water, and much harder to swim in. The youngsters found some little turtles sunning themselves on a log. When the whispering began, I knew that they were planning to keep them in the boat for the rest of the summer. How awful to have to face up to a thing like that, feeling as limp as I did! Then, fortunately, John's turtle bit his finger. When I heard him say sternly to it, "You are very rude, you can go right back to your mother," I knew that the problem was partially solved. But I would certainly have to keep an eye on Peter, or a turtle would turn up in the boat later.

Peter and John went exploring along the deer-trail on the edge of the lake. The two little naked boys suddenly began dancing up and down on the shore. "We found a dugout, we found a dugout!" Jan ran over to investigate. More shouts, and I ran too. It was long and very old, but it floated. It didn't take us long with our knives to fashion paddles out of this and that. Then, lunch-pail tucked in the bow, we paddled down the lake towards a low rocky point about a mile away. The dugout leaked quite a bit, and finally Peter and John had to take turns bailing with the lunch-pail. The loon was having hysterics now. Probably its wife and nest were hidden in the reeds that filled a little bay. The water was smooth as a looking-glass, and our reflection followed along under us as though we were hinged together. I would have liked to linger on that lake, but the water in the dugout was gaining on us, and it seemed expedient, as Captain Vancouver would have said, to make the shore.

There were signs that deer had been browsing in behind the rocky point, where maples overhung the cropped green grass. They would lie there in the shade on a hot afternoon, and their spotted babies would be hidden in the bracken beyond. How can a mother deer stand the constant alert for prowling bears or cougars? A doe's ears are always turning this way and that, tuning in on the slightest sound — smelling the wind for a betraying scent. I seldom had to tune in for anything worse than a turtle that might bite.

We turned the dugout over to dry while we ate our lunch on the shelving rock. We tried to caulk the crack with pine-needles and pitch. It was a long, long crack, but half a crack is better than a whole crack. Paddling back with the bits of this and that was harder than before — but bailing was reduced by half.

It was an effort in that limp state to have to squeeze through the pale-green tunnel again . . . . Then the children cornered a ten-inch trout by damming up its escape route. The trout never had a chance against three pairs of hands. I got tired of waiting while they planned further strategy. Telling them that I would light a fire on the beach, and bring the supper things ashore, I pushed ahead, and finally broke through to the beach, head first.

I lighted a fire and piled it up with bark — estimating that in an hour's time there would be a glowing bed of embers, just right for broiling trout.

It was the sound of their voices that woke me up. All smiling broadly . . . they actually had caught three more.

"That little one is John's," Peter announced, "because he can't eat as much."

"I can so — I'm just starved."

"Well, Jan and Peter have to clean them," I said, and took him out to the boat with me to prevent murder.

We always carried a rack for broiling fish. Soon they were spluttering and browning over a perfect fire, which I raked over between two flat stones. We built it up with more driftwood, which is always piled high at the top of the beaches on the British Columbia coast.

No one had any desire to fool around that evening. John fell asleep before it was even dark. The Northern Lights were edging this way . . . and that way . . . across the northern sky — reaching up above us — white and elusive, then retreating hurriedly down to the horizon.

It wasn't until Jan suddenly said, "Mummy, where's the dinghy?" that my spirit returned to its limp body.

I didn't actually have to swim — but very nearly. Somebody had committed the sin of sins — not tied it properly. I didn't ask. I didn't probe too deeply within myself — evidently a certain amount of salt is better than too little.

Shiners

 LEFT THE CHILDREN LYING ON THEIR STOMACHS ON THE float, fishing for shiners with thread and a bent pin. Shiners are little glittering fishes that like to congregate under wharfs or floats. They are thin, but almost round in profile.

When I rowed back later the children all started shouting to me as soon as I was within ear-shot.

"Mine did it first! Mine did it first! It did too, Jan." That was

Peter's voice.

I finally made myself heard. "If Peter's did, whatever it did, first — then let him tell me, whatever it did, first."

"My fish borned a baby," he brought out triumphantly.

"Mine kept borning and borning them," added John with scorn. "I just squeezed it."

"Anyway, it's perfectly true," said Jan, "and they can swim right away. We'll show you."

I waited while they baited up their pins with bits of sea-worm, and lay down to catch more shiners — dangling the bait in front of the seeking mouths. I sat there full of superior knowledge. I have several times caught salmon that had been feeding heavily among the brit, and have had them regurgitate a minnow that was quite able to swim away; pressed it again in getting the hook out — and another small Jonah had made the world. I would wait until they showed me, and then I would explain to them the habits of fish.

They waited until they had each caught a shiner, then crouched there waiting for the miracle to happen.

"Squeeze them," finally ordered Jan.

They squeezed them . . . . From the vent of each shiner came forth a perfectly formed silver baby. They were slim and narrow, not round and deep like their mothers. The second they were put in the water they darted to the bottom — to the weeds and safety. John kept on squeezing his, and his fish went on borning babies just as he had said. But each next baby was more transparent than the last; and they began to look like vague little ghosts with all their inner workings showing through. When you dropped them in the water they seemed all bewildered — and in seconds the big shiners closed in and swallowed them at a gulp, and eagerly waited around for more. I stopped John then, and explained that they were not ready to be born yet. That their mother probably let only one out each day, when it was properly finished and had all its instincts and was able to fend for itself in the big sea. Un-doubtedly — now that I knew — these shiner babies were being born all the time, at certain seasons. Perhaps their mothers were wise and only borned them in the dark night — then tiny phos-phorescent streaks would dart for the seaweed. Then the awful thought reared its head — did the mothers know their own babies?

Or did the babies have to elude the tigerish pounce of their own mother? It didn't bear thinking about.

When we got back to Little House in the fall, I would find out from the "Encyclopædia Britannica (1885)," just what it had to say about all this. Perhaps, for a change, I'd be able to tell it something it didn't know. After all, "Encyclopædia Britannica (1885)" states quite calmly, in black print, that malaria comes from the bad night air. Then I remembered my own little lecture, which fortunately had never been delivered. I conceded in my mind that we all make mistakes.

"Encyclopædia Britannica (1885)". . . .Yes, it knew all about viviparous fish — these shiners, as we called them, are a kind of rock perch. They and many others of that species are viviparous.

A Fish We Remember

E HAD TUCKED INTO THE LITTLE COVE AT THE NORTH end of Denman Island for the night, with no intention of staying over the next day. We had made a fire on the north-east beach, the only place there was any beach left above a very high tide. It was a still, quiet evening, and when it was dark the salmon started rising to the light that our fire cast on the calm water. Peter was feverishly carving a spear and hardening its point in the fire — just in case a fish came close enough to the little rocky point.

Off the end of Denman Island there is a great sandy bar that extends more than half a mile to the north and more than four miles west, almost to Cape Lazo. Plain sand would not be such a menace, but all the shallows are strewn with great boulders, which I think must wander all over the place in big winds. Just as you can move a boulder out of your garden by tucking more soil underneath it with the crowbar until it moves slowly but surely up to the surface, in the same way the big waves and the sand shift the boulders here and there.

It means going a long way round to Cape Lazo, to get past this sandy bar. If you try to cut through, you are suddenly surrounded by a maze of boulders. Every time you turn to avoid one, another

23

steps directly in front of you to block your way. In other summers you may have taken fixes on distant points or trees, and think you have worked out a passage. But the boulders have anticipated this — and have spent the intervening time inching their way into your supposed channel. At low tide there is perhaps six feet of water over the sand — sometimes more, sometimes less — but no one ever knows how much over the boulders.

A salmon rises and splashes in the fire-light, and then a seal surfaces with a loud snort. Peter, who has been standing on the rock with his spear poised for the last half-hour, groans, "Missed, just by inches." We all laugh, for it had been at least six feet.

Then I hurry everyone off to bed. Peter is crying because there will never be another chance like this. I who knew he never had a chance at all, console him by saying we will tie a heavy fish-line to it next time and he can cast the spear. A minute later he is laughing about the seal who had snorted because it had also missed the fish by inches.

I had planned to leave after breakfast and cut across to the mainland and up into Desolation Sound. And here I was gazing out over low tide on the sand-flats — the sea like glass and not a cloud in the sky; and surely after lunch would do just as well . . . . The youngsters sat there watching me anxiously, with deep sighs . . . . Then — they somehow knew before I did myself that we were going to stay, and I had to hurry up with the proviso: "Just until after lunch."

The tide must have been slack as well as low, for not a ripple nor a current stirred the surface of the water as we drifted silently over the sandy bottom and the surprised boulders. I just gave a gentle pull on the oars now and then . . . trying to blend ourselves in with the life of the sand-dwellers below.

Big red crabs with enormous claws would sidle across at an angle — making for the shelter of a boulder. We didn't know who their enemies were. Perhaps they didn't know who we were. We must have appeared like strange two-headed beasts to them — our faces joined nose to nose with our reflections in the water.

Bands of silvery minnows darted in unison — first here, then there. Some unknown mass signal seemed to control them — like sand-pipers flying low over the edge of a beach — the fluid concerted movement, concave edge changing to convex, and then

vice versa . . . . Or crows at some unknown signal dropping hel-
ter-skelter, head over heels, down through the air towards earth
and destruction . . . then as suddenly resuming their flight on
normal wings like perfectly sane crows. With the minnows we
could see that it was probably a preservation idea — they and their
shadows escaping bigger shadows and threatening dangers. But
who gives the signal and how is it made?

"Look! Look!" in whispers, first from one and then the others.
I could see on my side of the dinghy, but not on John's. Jan up in
the bow had a sea of her own — Peter's end, particularly his.

Suddenly, on my side, suspended perfectly motionless about
four feet down in the shadow cast by the dinghy, was a strange
fish — as though there by intent, waiting for us.

"Ss-s-s-se-e," I hissed, pointing carefully . . . and all the crew
hung, suspended motionless and precariously, over the edge —
all eyes focused on the fish.

It was about two feet long, shaped rather like a salmon, but
there the resemblance ended. This fish was a pale cream colour,
laced over with half-inch bands of old gold in a large diamond
pattern. Its eyes were dark, large and oval. Dark folds or eyelids
opened and shut, opened and shut . . . . It lay there chewing, or
was it the gills like a jaw-line that gave it the ruminating appearance?

Something hadn't liked this cream-and-gold fish — one piece
of its tail was gone, and one of its side-fins was torn and ragged
— all rather dishevelled and routed looking.

It just lay there quietly — raising and lowering its large oval
eyelids; we suspended in our dinghy, it suspended in the safety of
our shadow. That of course was probably why it was there — for
protection.

Then a seal broke water and the glassy surface was in a turmoil.
When it had quietened, our cream-and-gold fish had gone.

"Probably the same seal that ruined my fish last night." said
Peter.

Then he and Jan slid into the water and tried to see how many
boulders they could touch before they got to shore.

The tide was rising and the water still so glassy that, when we
left after lunch, we cut across the bar of sand and the boulders
with John and Peter lying flat in the bow. Then we ambled across

25

the twenty-five-mile stretch of open water towards Savary Island over on the mainland. We fooled around and tried to find Mystery Reef and couldn't. Then we moved on up to the Ragged Islands for supper, and perhaps the night. I think we all felt groggy with the glare off the water, and it was good to get in close to the cliffs in the shade.

There seemed to be a slight, hardly noticeable swell as I cooked supper with one foot up on the steering-seat as usual. The air was almost oppressively still, and my face was burning like fire. A tugboat tooted at the entrance to the cove; he wanted to tie up just where we were anchored. Why on earth did they want to tie up on an evening like this? Then the pieces began to fall into place, and I snatched Jan's bathing-cap off the barometer where it had hung all day. The glass was down to 29 and it had been over 31 at breakfast time.

I told Jan to take over the supper and handed the table that lived on top of the engine-box to Peter, and told them to carry on. I waved at the tug, which tooted again, and I pulled up the anchor. If we were going to ride out a south-easter, we would do it up in Desolation Sound in the cove on Mink Island, where there was water and room to move around — not in a ragged cove with a restless boom.

Before we reached Mink Island, the mares' tails in the sky were trailing wildly. Then it was dark and the waves at our heels were throwing the phosphorus out ahead of them.

The stars only showed now and then, and it was hard to find the entrance to the cove. I sent Jan up on deck with the flashlight — and after a little while we made out the sheltering points and crept thankfully in and round the turn to drop our hook.

Cougar

E NEVER STARTED OFF AT THE BEGINNING OF THE summer expecting trouble or exciting things — at least, not after the first couple of years. Then, I think, we were looking for adventures. Later, when we found out what adventures were like, we tried to avoid them, but they came anyway. So, after that, except for "exercising due care," as the early explorers said, we neither anticipated them nor tried to avoid them. We just accepted them as a normal part of the increasing number of miles we logged every summer.

This summer we had exercised due care by leaving our Gordon setter at home. Other summers she had always come with us — enduring it rather than liking it, I think. She always had to tow behind in the dinghy, unless it was really rough. If we didn't have the sense to know when that stage was reached — she always did. Instead of lying quietly asleep on her sack in the stern-sheets of the dinghy, she would suddenly sit straight up. Her nose would swing from side to side, trying to decide what was blowing up, what the barometer was doing. She would look at the waves on one side of her, then on the other — turning over in her mind how long she would wait before she made her demands.

When the first spray from a slightly bigger wave reached her, she would put on her long-suffering, determined look and move up into the bow of the dinghy. Then the dinghy would yaw — first to one side and then to the other — Pam ageing visibly with each swing. She was completely deaf to every command to go back to her proper seat.

"Mummy," Peter would plead, "she's terrified!" Wily old Pam — salt-water crocodile tears streaming down her face.

"All right . . . ." I would say grudgingly — knowing exactly what would happen at the next stage, when the waves got a little bigger. "Pull her in."

Everyone sprang to the rope, while I slowed the boat down. Before they could pull the dinghy to within four feet, Pam would gather her feet together and, with a magnificent leap, land lightly on the after-deck — smiling broadly. Everybody patted her, everybody loved her. She curled up happily on the coil of rope and went to sleep.

Another half-hour and she sat up again — bolt upright. No need for her to look at the barometer — she knew. "When are we going to get out of this?" her eyes and set of her mouth demanded. I was standing up to steer now, and the youngsters were playing cards on the little table that was wedged in between the two bunks. There was a shriek of "Pam!" One leap had landed her in the middle of the cards. The next up against the back of my legs in the only few square inches left on the deck of the cockpit. She didn't dare smile this time. Nor did anyone dare pat her.

John climbed up onto the steering seat beside me. "She's very bad, isn't she?" he said. "Is it very rough?"

"Oh, no," I said. "Pam is just being silly. See that point over there — we go in behind that."

"Where?" asked Jan, moving up beside me.

"My, it's rough!" said Peter, pushing in too. "Pam always knows, doesn't she?"

"How am I supposed to steer, with a dog lying on my feet, and my silly crew jamming both my arms?" I demanded.

But all that was not why I decided to leave her at home this time. It was what happened last summer on our way north. We had anchored in Melanie Cove off Desolation Sound for a few days to enjoy the warm swimming. Then it clouded up and started to rain. The mountains back of Desolation Sound seem at times to be a favourite rendezvous for clouds that are undecided where to go. They drape themselves forlornly on all the high peaks, trail themselves down the gorges, and then unload themselves as rain on the sea at the mountains' feet.

Pam had either to sleep on shore at night or else in the dinghy, which she prefers. That night it was so wet that I moved the boat over against the shore, on the opposite side from the copper stain on the cliff. There is an old shed there raised on short posts that is nice and dry underneath. Pam had spent wet nights there before, so she knew the place and raised no objections. The children rowed her ashore, fixed up a bed of bracken for her, and left her with a dish of food.

Then we got the Coleman stove going and supper on, and were soon dry and comfortable. It was surprising how comfortable we could be on a rainy day in that little boat. With the heavy canvas side-curtains buttoned securely down, the back curtain stretched open at an angle for fresh air — the two-burner stove on top of the steering seat would soon dry all the inside of the boat and us. We got the sleeping bags out early, and everything straightened. Unless we were sitting round a fire on the beach or rocks we always turned in before it was quite dark. It was a dead calm night, with not a sound except the hiss of the falling rain and the plop of the raindrops as they hit the sea and made little spurting craters.

28

I don't know how late it was when something wakened me. I listened . . . trying to orientate myself . . . trying to remember just where we were anchored. Then Pam whined — and there was something desperate in the tone. I groped for the flashlight and unfastened the curtain beside me. It was still pouring. I shone the light towards the shed — but there was no sign of Pam where they had made her bed. Another whine from somewhere nearer us than the shed. I swung the beam down the shore to the edge of the water. Another whine, and I had to lower it still farther . . . . There, up to her neck in the sea, was Pam.

"Pam!" I said. "What *is* the matter?"

She glanced nervously towards the shore; then turned back and whined. Obviously she wanted to come on board; and obviously there wasn't an inch of room. The dinghy, where she often slept in fine weather, was half-full of water — and the sky was giving us all it had. Pam didn't like bears — but a black bear wouldn't bother her, tucked under a shed like that. I coaxed and pleaded, and finally ordered her back to bed. Slowly . . . so slowly . . . she splashed back and got under the shed. There she sat — glancing first over one shoulder, then the other. I flashed the light all over the woods. I called. I talked loudly to scare away any bear that might be around. Finally, Pam went farther under the shed and curled up on her bracken bed. I hushed the questioning crew back to sleep, and went to sleep myself.

It was about six o'clock when I awoke again. The clouds had broken up and a shafted sun was trying to disperse the mist. I unfastened the curtain and looked towards the shed. I needn't have looked so far. There in the water, up to her neck, was Pam — looking like a sad seal that had just surfaced. How long she had been there, we didn't know. We bailed out the dinghy, and two of the youngsters rowed ashore and took Pam off. I made them take her across to an island on the other side and race her up and down to get her warm, while I cooked a big pot of rolled oats for her. With heaps of sugar and evaporated milk, that must have been the morning of a dog's heaven. Then we put her on deck in the sun. She was warm and dry and happy. But in spite of all the questioning, she wouldn't tell anyone why she had done such a foolish thing.

After breakfast we pulled up the anchor and went round to

Laura Cove to get some eggs from Phil, the old Frenchman who lived there. I told him what had happened in the night, and said I supposed it must have been a bear.

"Dat weren't no bear," said Phil, emphatically. "A dog don't act that way about a bear. Dat were a cougar, an' I suppose it will be atter my goats next."

Pam got badly spoiled after that. She was a heroine — she had outwitted a cougar.

On our way south again, six weeks later, we called in at Phil Lavine's again. As soon as he saw our boat, he hurried down to the float. Hardly waiting to say, "Hello," he started off excitedly:

"Say, you remember dat night your dog stayed in de water all night? Well, de next night dat cougar got my old billy-goat on dat little island where I keep 'im." He pointed to a small island not very far from where we stood. He had heard the old goat bleating or screaming at about four in the morning, and knew that something was wrong. He grabbed his gun; ran down to the float and rowed across. There was a great round boulder on the beach, and he could see the head and shoulders of the goat sticking out on one side. The goat was lying on the ground and he thought it might have broken its leg, for it kept making this awful noise. He stepped out of the boat and started towards it — then turned back and picked up his gun.

"Atter dat dog of yours I weren't taking no chances," he said. He skirted out and around the boulder . . . . There, hanging on to the hind-end of the goat, was a full-sized cougar.

"I got 'im first shot — between de eyes . . . den I 'ad to shoot de goat."

We followed him up to the woodshed, where he had the skin pegged out on the wall. It was a big one, eight or nine feet long. Pam gave one sniff at it and slunk back to the boat.

"See!" said Phil, "dat ain't no bear-acting!"

I realized it wasn't — Pam barks hysterically when she runs from a bear.

"Don't you let dos kids of your sleep on shore wid de dog at night — ever. De cougar would be atter de dog, but de kids might get hurt too."

Nothing would have induced any of them to sleep on shore again, with or without the dog — after seeing that skin.

Desolation

E BUCKED A STRONG TIDE AND WEST WIND, AND RAN for ten hours that day before we finally turned in by Sarah Point. From there we set a straight course for Mink Island, where there is good shelter and fresh water from a small fall.

It was good to be on land again. We made a fire on the sloping rock, and while waiting for it to burn down to embers we swam and played around in the warm water. I had just started to think about supper when a boat we knew came into the bay and presented us with a chunk of out-of-season venison. We cut it into steaks and broiled it, then ate it in our hands on big slices of bread — hoping that it would look and smell like lamb, if any unfriendly boat came into the bay.

Vancouver had named this part of the coast Desolation Sound. On their return from Jervis Inlet — tired, disappointed, and out of food — and when they turned south to rejoin their ships, they were very surprised to find two Spanish vessels at anchor off Burrard Inlet. The *Sutil*, under command of Senor Don Galiano, and the *Mexicana*, under Senor Don Valdes.

Vancouver says: "I had experienced no small degree of mortification in finding the external shores of the gulf had already been visited and examined a few miles beyond where my researches had extended."

Later, the *Discovery* and the *Chatham* and the two Spanish vessels joined forces and sailed up Malaspina Strait together. They evidently entered Desolation Sound after dark and in the rain, and had drifted and been blown around helplessly, unable to get any soundings. Finally, they ended up on the north side of an island, where they all managed to anchor in thirty-two fathoms.

The next morning they found themselves "about half a mile from the shores of a high rocky island, surrounded by a detached and broken country, whose general appearance was very inhospitable. Stupendous rocky mountains rising almost perpendicularly from the sea principally composed the north-west, north, and east quarters." Vancouver mentions that they could not trace the range of mountains that they had seen stretching far to the north-west of Jervis Inlet. The mountains in Desolation Sound are just on the edge of that range — as he half supposed.

The morning was fine, and their small boats were sent off exploring in all directions. But in the afternoon the wind started to blow from the south-east, attended with heavy squalls and much rain. Their anchors dragged off into eighty fathoms, and they had to heave them up and make for an anchorage and rendezvous that one of the small boats had been sent to find.

It took them until six o'clock to get the four ships safely anchored in Teakerne Arm on Redonda Island.

We cruised around the next morning, and finally found and identified their rocky island as the present Kinghorn Island. Then, never having been in Teakerne Arm, we ran up there to spend the night. We found it rather a delightful place: high rocky shores, two and three thousand feet in height, except over in one bay to the north where a waterfall leaps seventy feet down into the sea. It comes from lakes directly behind the falls, and the water is warm, with a more or less sandy beach at the foot.

The ships were anchored in there for two weeks while the small boats explored in all directions. Archibald Menzies, the botanist, says: "They rowed over to the falls every day and used it more or less like a resort."

Captain Vancouver, who seems to have stayed on board the *Discovery* making up his notes and maps, was once more depressed — I suppose after finding that one more inlet, Toba, did not cut through the mountains.

He says: "Our situation here was an arm of the Sound leading to the north-west a little more than half a mile wide, presenting as gloomy and dismal an aspect as nature could well be supposed to exhibit. Our residence here was truly forlorn — an awful silence pervaded the gloomy forest while animated nature seemed to have deserted the neighbouring country, whose soil afforded only a few wild onions, some samphire, and here and there some bushes bearing a scanty crop of indifferent berries. Nor was the sea more favourable to our wants — the steep shore prevented the use of the seine, and not a fish on the bottom could be tempted to take the hook."

Mr. Johnstone and his party had gone up to the head of Toba Inlet. On their way back they explored Prideaux Haven, a collection of small islands and coves in the north-east corner of Desolation Sound. There they found a deserted Indian village. Judging from the number of shacks they thought it must have held about three hundred persons. It was built on a high rocky peninsula with perpendicular rock sides, connected to the mainland by a narrow neck of land with a plank bridge up to the rock. The Indians had built a wooden platform on the face of the rock in front of the houses and projecting out over the sheer cliff, making it impossible for enemies to climb up. Examining this site the sailors were suddenly assailed with legions of ferocious fleas. The fleas were so bad that the men rushed up to their necks in the water to try to get rid of them. But it wasn't until they boiled their clothes that they succeeded. They supposed that the Indians had abandoned the village on account of the fleas. In all our summers up the coast we have always found the Indian villages empty. Most of them are winter villages to which the Indians come back after being off in their dugouts all summer.

Captain Vancouver, who had been much puzzled by the tides in all these regions, as reported by his young gentlemen, came to the conclusion that they were flooding in from the north as well, which must denote open sea to the north-west. Accordingly, he sent Mr. Johnstone and his boat up to the north-west to discover where this flood-tide came from.

Mr. Johnstone worked his way through the Yuculta Rapids and all the other intricate passages; and eventually into a narrow, open passage that led him right through to Alleviation Island, from where he was able to get a clear view of the Pacific beyond. That being what he had been sent out to find, he turned back. Now, instead of all the intricate passages by which he had come north, he sailed straight down through the narrow, open passage he had found, until he reached the latitude of the ships. He cut across to them at the north end of Quadra Island.

After hearing Mr. Johnstone's report, Captain Vancouver said good-bye to the Spaniards, and with the *Discovery* and the *Chatham* made for Cape Mudge on the south end of Quadra Island. From there they sailed up the now-called Johnstone Strait to the open Pacific. On the way they passed a village in Menzies Bay — twenty canoes filled with Indians observed to be highly painted. "The faces of some were entirely white, some red, black, or lead colour. While others were adorned with several colours. Most of them had their hair decorated with the down of young sea-fowl." (Down in the hair was a sign of peace.)

Up at the Nimkish River, just before they came out into the open Pacific, they visited the Indians in a large village. They were friendly, and well acquainted with white men, there being a trail from their village across Vancouver Island to Nootka on the west coast, where there was a Spanish fort and trading-post. The Indians at Nimkish had firearms. Vancouver mentions that a number of these Kwakiutl Indians had heavy black beards — proof, I should think, that the Spaniards and Russians had been on the north-west coast for many years.

We were not exactly trying to follow Vancouver's route — we already knew practically all the places he had been to. But we had a copy of his diary on board and we were filling in the few gaps in our knowledge. We spent a couple of nights in Teakerne Arm — the waterfall and the lake being a big attraction. Then, wanting to put in time while we waited for better tides in the Yuculta Rapids, we followed the course that Vancouver had taken with his two ships over to Cape Mudge on Quadra Island.

They went by Sutil Channel, a wide, deep channel that leads fairly directly to Quadra Island and then south to Cape Mudge.

We followed by a small-boat channel five miles farther north. The whole area lies between the Yuculta Rapids on the north — up against the mainland, and the Seymour Narrows and Discovery Passage on the south — up against Vancouver Island, covering roughly four hundred square miles. It is almost completely filled with large islands that seem to have split apart from each other like a disintegrating ice-floe, and serve as a great baffle-plate in the centre of the conflicting tides. The narrow leads in between the island have revealing names — Surge Narrows, Hole-in-the-Wall, Okisollo Channel. The narrow boat-passage that we had come through was, as the *Coast Pilot* had warned us, choked with drying rocks. But we knew that the local people sometimes used it if they had missed the tide in Hole-in-the-Wall. Hole-in-the-Wall is a rapid that runs from eight to ten knots, and with practically no slack it just slaps round from one direction to the other. Entrance to it is from the Yuculta side. Okisollo Channel has two rapids, and opens out from Seymour Narrows side. Surge Narrows, which is south-east of the other two, is probably the worst. The channel there turns abruptly at right angles and forces the stream, which runs at nine knots, between small islands with dangerous cross-currents. None of these, the tide-book warns, is available to other than small local boats.

It seemed to us to be a place of great risks and, probably, much luck. Yet we knew that in the winter-time the scattered people from the Yuculta district would pile their fish-boats full of people, from the smallest baby to the oldest grandmother, and work through Hole-in-the-Wall and Okisollo with the tide to attend a dance over on the Seymour Narrows side — a dance that would last until Sunday afternoon and the turn of a tide. Then, later, the Yuculta people would hold a dance in the store at Stuart Island; and from all directions, Hole-in-the-Wall, the Arran Rapids, and the Yucultas, the fish-boats would surge into the Stuart Island wharf.

We spent the whole day avoiding drying rocks, or being pushed by the tide in directions we didn't want to go, and holing up in little bays until we could move in the direction we wanted to. It was late when the tide hurried us out of those lonely waters into Sutil Channel — deep and wide and free of rocks. We speeded up and headed for Quadra — the largest of this group of islands that plugged the channel. It is a big island — twenty miles long, and the side we were on was to the north. It seemed desolate and dreary. We turned down towards Cape Mudge where there was more chance of shelter for the night.

We were passing a very uninviting bay, grey, small firs dripping moss, a boulder shore with drift-logs at the top, when . . .

"Mummy!" said Jan, in a horrified voice. "What is that?"

We crowded over to her side of the boat to see what she was pointing at. A very large bird with a big wingspread, red head and neck, was circling low above the beach. As we watched, two more rose slowly and silently from behind the logs into the air. And then the three of them, red heads on long red necks, after peering balefully at our boat, slid silently off into the dark forest.

"There is a horrid smell!" whispered Peter.

There was — the sickly, searching smell of something very dead . . . not fish.

"What were they?" whispered Jan.

"Vultures," I whispered.

"What?" whispered John.

"Vultures!" I shouted, to break the spell that an unknown horror had cast over us. "Just vultures."

"I can't bear them!" said Jan, getting back her voice. "Why didn't they make any noise?"

"What's a vulture?" broke in Peter.

I had never seen a vulture before. I didn't even know there were any on the coast of British Columbia. I thought they lived in deserts. Evidently they are things that don't need any introduction, you just guess, when you see them.

I speeded up to get away from the smell. We still had to find an anchorage for the night; we hadn't eaten yet, and it would soon be dark.

"I see an old home in there," said Peter presently.

I slowed down and took the binoculars from him. It seemed worth investigating. There was a small island in the bay to one side of the point where the house was. There wouldn't be a house in this desolate place unless there was a shelter for a boat. Jan went up to the bow, and we drew in towards the little island.

Jan held out her arm and motioned, and I swung towards the left of the island, then through a narrow opening between the island and the shore. It opened out into a little bay with a beach. Both sheltered by the island — and there was enough water for anchorage. In a south-easter you might have the whole Gulf of Georgia trying to get in too — but it would do for tonight.

I couldn't let out very much chain — there was not much room to swing. I could hardly see the brown house, lying quiet among the trees. There was no light. Was anyone listening? If we called out "Is anyone there?" would anyone answer?

I wouldn't let the children land on the beach. They had to be content with the little island, while I cooked the supper.

I didn't have a very good night — a breeze came up from the south-east, and we slopped a bit. I wasn't worrying about it — but a change of any kind in the night always rouses me. But I kept thinking of the vultures and wondering what had been behind the log . . . and that wasn't conducive to sleep. And the brown house I could no longer see, stood there, listening . . . .

After breakfast we went on shore to explore. Up three or four wooden steps from the beach; then along a gravel path bordered on both sides by lilac bushes. There had once been lawns, and neglected flower-beds circled the house. A verandah ran round three sides reached by a flight of steps. We skirted round to the other side. Here the lawn sloped steeply to the sea, and there was a ground-floor room with door and windows. The door stood open, so we looked in. A kitchen stove stood there, chairs, and a dining-table. On the table, a plate with a knife and a piece of bread. Had someone taken to the woods when they heard our boat?

We backed out cautiously and, with one eye on the woods, went round the house and up the steps onto the verandah. There was no glass in any of the windows, but each one was securely covered with small-mesh chickenwire. I first thought that someone must have used the house for chickens. But looking through a window I saw that the wire hadn't been for chickens. There were odds and ends of furniture, and the floor was littered with torn letters and pamphlets, otherwise quite clean. I tried the one door, and it opened. We went in . . . . The windows at the back of the house were covered with the wire too. Someone had evidently been trying to keep something either in or out — but which, or what?

I picked up a couple of pamphlets from the floor. They were all about the life of the spirit after death, and how to get into communication, published by some society of psychical research. Most of the torn letters were written by people of education. Then I found some pages from a diary, written just the last winter. It fooled me at first — it was rather beautiful, rather like James Joyce in parts. Then suddenly, some sentence made me realize that the mind of the writer was on a very, very strange plane . . . .

I had straightened up — thinking that I would take the pages with me and read them later, away from the "heavy, heavy hangs over your head" atmosphere — when I noticed a framed picture on the wall, a picture of someone wrapped in white lying on a couch. Above the wrapped figure hovered a strange white cloud of vapour. Underneath was written, "Authentic photograph of spirit leaving body after death."

I left, opening the door only a little, and shutting it quickly

37

behind me. I knew now the reason for the wire — the diarist had been trying to keep something he had trapped in there from getting out.

Mike

HE FIRST TIME WE MET MIKE MUST HAVE BEEN THE VERY first time we anchored in Melanie Cove. It was blowing a heavy south-easter outside, so we had turned into Desolation Sound and run right up to the eastern end. There the chart showed some small coves called Prideaux Haven. The inner one, Melanie Cove, turned out to be wonderful shelter in any wind.

We anchored over against a long island with a shelving rock shore. The children tumbled into the dinghy and rowed ashore to collect wood for the evening bonfire, while I started the supper. Away in at the end of the cove we could see what appeared to be fruit trees of some kind, climbing up a side hill. It was in August, and our mouths started watering at the thought of green apple sauce and dumplings. There was no sign of a house of any kind, no smoke. It might even be a deserted orchard. After supper we would go in and reconnoitre.

We were just finishing our supper when a boat came out of the end of the cove with a man standing up rowing — facing the bow and pushing forward on the oars. He was dressed in the usual logger's outfit — heavy grey woollen undershirt above, heavy black trousers tucked into high leather boots. As I looked at him when he came closer, Don Quixote came to mind at once. High pointed forehead and mild blue eyes, a fine long nose that wandered down his face, and a regular Don Quixote moustache that drooped down at the ends. When he pulled alongside we could see the cruel scar that cut in a straight line from the bridge of his nose — down the nose inside the flare of the right nostril, and down to the lip.

"Well, well, well," said the old man — putting his open hand over his face just below the eyes, and drawing it down over his nose and mouth, closing it off the end of his chin — a gesture I got to know so well in the summers to come.

"One, two, three, four, five," he counted, looking at the children.

He wouldn't come aboard, but he asked us to come ashore after supper and pick some apples; there were lots of windfalls. We could move the boat farther into the cove, but not beyond the green copper stain on the cliff. Later, I tossed a couple of magazines in the dinghy and we rowed towards where we had seen him disappear. We identified the copper stain for future use, rounded a small sheltering island, and there, almost out of sight up the bank, stood a little cabin — covered with honeysuckle and surrounded by flowers and apple trees. We walked with him along the paths, underneath the overhanging apple-branches. He seemed to know just when each tree had been planted, and I gathered that it had been a slow process over the long years he had lived there.

Except for down at the far end, where the little trellis-covered bridge dripped with grapes, the land all sloped steeply from the sea and up the hillside to the forest. Near the cabin he had terraced it all — stone-walled, and flower-bordered. Old-fashioned flowers — mignonette and sweet-williams, bleeding-hearts and bachelor's buttons. These must have reached back into some past of long ago, of which at that time I knew nothing. But beauty, which had certainly been achieved, was not the first purpose of the terraces — the first purpose was apple trees.

He had made one terrace behind the house first — piled stones, carted seaweed and earth until he had enough soil for the first trees. From there, everything had just gradually grown. Down at the far end, where terraces were not necessary, the trees marched up the hillside in rows to where the eight-foot sapling fence surrounded the whole place. "The deer jump anything lower," said Mike, when I commented on the amount of time and work it must have taken. Then he added, "Time doesn't mean anything to me. I just work along with nature, and in time it is finished."

Mike sent the children off to gather windfalls — all they could find — while he showed me his cabin. There was a bookshelf full of books across one end of the main room, and an old leather chair. A muddle of stove, dishpan and pots at the other end, and a table. Then down three steps into his winter living-room, half below ground level. "Warmer in winter," he explained. He saw us down to the boat, and accepted the two magazines. Then he went back to the cabin to get a book for me, which he said I might like to read if I were going to be in the cove for a few days.

"Stoort sent it to me for Christmas," he said. I felt that I should have known who Stoort was. I couldn't see the title, but I thanked him. The children were laden with apples — and full of them, I was sure.

Back in the boat, I looked at the book by flashlight. It was *Why be a Mud Turtle*, by Stewart Edward White. I looked inside — on the fly-leaf was written, "To my old friend Andrew Shuttler, who most emphatically is not a mud turtle."

During the next couple of days I spent a lot of time talking to old Mike, or Andrew Shuttler — vouched for by Stewart Edward White as being, most emphatically, worth talking to. The children were happy swimming in the warm water, eating apples, and picking boxes of windfalls for Mike to take over to the logging camp at Deep Bay.

In between admiring everything he showed me around the place — I gradually heard the story of some of his past, and how he first came to Melanie Cove. He had been born back in Michigan in the States. After very little schooling he had left school to go to work. When he was big enough he had worked in the Michigan woods as a logger — a hard, rough life. I don't know when, or how, he happened to come to British Columbia. But here again, he had worked up the coast as a logger.

"We were a wild, bad crowd," mused Mike — looking back at his old life, a far-away look in his blue eyes. Then he told of the fight he had had with another logger.

"He was out to get me . . . . I didn't have much chance."

The fellow had left him for dead, lying in a pool of his own blood. Mike wasn't sure how long he had lain there — out cold. But the blood-soaked mattress had been all fly-blown when he came to.

"So it must have been quite some few days."

He had dragged himself over to a pail of water in the corner of the shack and drunk the whole pailful . . . then lapsed back into unconsciousness. Lying there by himself — slowly recovering.

"I decided then," said Mike, "that if that was all there was to life, it wasn't worth living; and I was going off somewhere by

40

myself to think it out."

So he had bought or probably pre-empted wild little Melanie Cove — isolated by 7,000-foot mountains to the north and east, and only accessible by boat. Well, he hadn't wanted neighbours, and everything else he needed was there. Some good alder bottom-land and a stream, and a sheltered harbour. And best of all to a logger, the south-east side of the cove rose steeply, to perhaps eight hundred feet, and was covered with virgin timber. So there, off Desolation Sound, Mike had built himself a cabin, hand-logged and sold his timber — and thought about life . . . .

He had been living there for over thirty years when we first blew into the cove. And we must have known him for seven or eight years before he died. He had started planting the apple trees years before — as soon as he had realized that neither the trees nor his strength would last forever. He had built the terraces, carted the earth, fed and hand-reared them. That one beside the cabin door — a man had come ashore from a boat with a pocket full of apples. Mike had liked the flavour, and heeled in his core beside the steps.

"Took a bit of nursing for a few years," said Mike. "Now, look at it. Almost crowding me out."

He took us up the mountain one day to where he had cut some of the timber in the early days, and to show us the huge stumps. He explained how one man alone could saw the trees by rigging up what he called a "spring" to hold the other end of the saw against the cut. And how if done properly, the big tree would drop onto the smaller trees you had felled to serve as skids, and would slide down the slope at a speed that sent it shooting out into the cove. He could remember the length of some of them, and how they had been bought for the big drydock down in Vancouver.

I got to know what books he had in the cabin. Marcus Aurelius, Epictetus, Plato, Emerson, among many others. Somebody had talked to him, over the years, and sent him books to help him in his search. He didn't hold with religion, but he read and thought and argued with everything he read. One summer I had on board a book by an East Indian mystic — a book much read down in the States. I didn't like it — it was much too materialistic to my way of thinking, using spiritual ways for material ends. I gave it to Mike to read, not saying what I thought of it, and wondered what

41

he would make of it. He sat in his easy chair out underneath an apple tree, reading for hour after hour . . . while I lay on the rocks watching the children swim, and reading one of his books.

He handed it back the next day — evidently a little embarrassed in case I might have liked it. He drew his hand down and over his face, hesitated . . . . Then:

"Just so much dope," he said apologetically. "All words — not how to think or how to live, but how to get things with no effort!"

I don't think anyone could have summed up that book better than the logger from Michigan.

Atlantic Monthly, Harper's — he loved them. I would leave him a pile of them. At the end of the summer, when we called in again, he would discuss all the articles with zest and intelligence.

Mike's own Credo, as he called it, was simple. He had printed it in pencil on a piece of cardboard, and had it hanging on his wall. He had probably copied it word for word from some book — because it expressed for him how he had learnt to think and live. I put it down here exactly as he had it.

"Look well of to-day — for it is the Life of Life. In its brief course lie all the variations and realities of your life — the bliss of growth, the glory of action, the splendour of beauty. For yesterday is but a dream, and To-morrow a vision. But To-day well lived makes every Yesterday a dream of happiness, and every To-morrow a vision of hope. For Time is but a scene in the eternal drama. So, look well of to-day, and let that be your resolution as you awake each morning and salute the New Dawn. Each day is born by the recurring miracle of Dawn, and each night reveals the celestial harmony of the stars. Seek not death in error of your life, and pull not upon yourself destruction by the work of your hands."

That was just exactly how Mike lived — day by day, working with nature. That was really how he had recovered from the fight years ago. And later how he had pitted the strength of one man against the huge trees — seven and eight feet in diameter and two hundred or more feet high. Just the right undercut; just the right angle of the saw; just the right spots to drive in the wedges — using nature as his partner. And if sometimes both he and nature failed, there was always the jack — a logger's jack of enormous size and strength that could edge a huge log the last critical inches to start the skid.

He lent his books to anyone who would read them, but the field was small. For a time there was a logging outfit in Deep Bay, three miles away. They used to buy his vegetables and fruit. Some of them borrowed his books. He talked and tried to explain some of his ideas to the old Frenchman in Laura Cove — old Phil Lavine, who was supposed to have killed a man back in Quebec. After Mike was dead, old Phil commented to me, almost with satisfaction, "All dem words, and 'e 'ad to die like all de rest of us!"

But the next year when we called in to see him, old Phil had built book-shelves on his wall — around and above his bunk, and on the shelves were all Mike's books. Phil was standing there proudly, thumbs hooked in his braces, while some people off a yacht looked at the titles and commented on his collection . . . . Phil the savant — Phil who could neither read nor write.

Among Mike's circle of friends — lumbermen, trappers, fishermen, people from passing boats that anchored in the cove — not many of them would have stayed long enough, or been able to appreciate the fine mind old Mike had developed for himself. And the philosophy he had acquired from all he had read in his search to find something that made life worth living.

I can't remember from whom I heard that Mike had died during the winter. When we anchored there the next year, the cove rang like an empty seashell. A great northern raven, which can carry on a conversation with all the intonations of the human voice, flew out from above the cabin, excitedly croaking, "Mike's dead! Mike's dead!" All the cliffs repeated it, and bandied it about.

The cabin had been stripped of everything — only a rusty stove and a litter of letters and cards on the floor. I picked up a card. On the back was written, "Apple time is here again, and thoughts of ripe apples just naturally make us think of philosophy and you." It was signed, "Betty Stewart Edward White."

Apple time was almost here again now, and the trees were laden. But apples alone were not enough for us. We needed old Mike to pull his hand down over his face in the old gesture, and to hear his — "Well, well, well! Summer's here, and here you are again!"

Indian Villages

THROTTLED DOWN THE ENGINE, LIFTED JOHN UP ON THE steering seat, and left the boat to drift idly under his care, while the rest of us unrolled the chart and tried to discover just where we were.

As far as the eye could see, islands, big and little, crowded all round us — each with its wooded slopes rising to a peak covered with wind blown firs; each edged with twisted junipers, scrub-oak and mosses, and each ready to answer immediately to any name we thought the chart might like it to have. To the north-east, the snow-capped mountains of the coast range reached with their jagged peaks for the summer sky. And north, south, east and west, among the maze of islands, winding channels lured and beckoned. That was what we had been doing all day — just letting our little boat carry us where she pleased.

But we were looking for old Indian villages, and we had to find out where we were. So we turned the chart this way and that way, trying to make it fit what lay before our eyes.

"We came through there, and along there, and up there," pointed Peter, whose sense of direction is fairly good.

So we swung a mountain a few degrees to the west.

But Jan, who is three years older, snorted, took her pencil and showed us — "This is where we saw the Indian spearing fish, and that is where we saw the Indian painting on the cliff."

So we meekly swung the mountain back again, and over to the east.

Then the channels began to have some definite direction, and the islands sorted themselves out — the right ones standing forward bold and green; the others retiring, dim and unwanted. We relieved John at the wheel; the other two climbed up into the bow to watch for reefs; and we began to make our way cautiously through the shallow, unknown waters that would eventually bring us to one of the Indian villages.

We were far north of our usual cruising ground this summer: in the waters of the Kwakiutl Indians, one of the West Coast tribes of Canada. Their islands lie among hundreds of other islands on the edge of Queen Charlotte Sound, well off the usual ship courses, and many of them accessible only through narrow confusing passages. In summer it is fairly quiet and sheltered; but in the spring and fall the big winds from the open Pacific sweep up the sound and through the islands, stunting and twisting the trees. And in winter cold winds blow down the great fiord that cuts eighty miles through the islands and mountains to the north-east. And at all times of the year, without any warning, comes the fog — soft, quiet, obliterating.

We had found an old stone hammer on our own land the winter before. It was shaped more like a pestle, which we thought it was. But trips to the museum, and books from the library, and a whole winter's reading, had made us familiar with the history and habits of these Indians. So we had made up our minds to spend part of the summer among the old villages with the big community houses, and try to recapture something of a Past that will soon be gone forever.

There is little habitation in those waters, beyond the occasional logging camp or trading centre hidden in some sheltered bay. The Indians living among these islands have the same setting that they have had for hundreds of years, and cling to many of their old customs. It seems to give the region a peculiar atmosphere belonging to the Past. Already we could feel it crowding closer. And the farther we penetrated into these waters the more we felt that we were living in a different age — had perhaps lived there before . . . perhaps dimly remembered it all.

Yesterday, we had passed a slender Indian dugout. An Indian was standing up in the bow, holding aloft a long fish-spear poised, ready to strike. His woman was crouched in the stern, balancing the canoe with her paddle — a high, sheer cliff behind them. Cliff, dugout, primitive man; all were mirrored in the still water beneath them. He struck — tossed the wriggling fish into the dugout, and resumed his pose. When was it that we had watched them? Yesterday? a hundred years ago? or just somewhere on that curve of Time?

Farther and farther into that Past we slipped. Down winding tortuous byways — strewn with reefs, fringed with kelp. Now and then, out of pity for our propeller, we poled our way through the cool, green shallows — slipping over the pointed groups of great starfish, all purple and red and blue; turning aside the rock cod

45

swimming with their lazy tails; making the minnows wheel and dart in among the sea grapes. In other stretches herons disputed our right-of-way with raucous cries, and bald-headed eagles stared silently from their dead tree perches. Once a mink shrieked and dropped his fish to flee, but turned to scream and defy us. Perhaps, as Peter suggested, he was a mother one.

We turned into more open water, flanked with bigger islands, higher hills.

"Mummy! Mummy! A whale!" shouted Jan, and almost directly ahead of us a grey whale blew and dived.

"Two whales! Two whales!" shrieked the whole crew, as a great black killer whale rose in hot pursuit, his spar fin shining in the sun. He smacked the water with his great flanged tail and dived after his prey — both heading directly our way.

We were safe behind a reef before they rose again. The grey whale hardly broke water; but we could see the killer's make-believe eye glare, and his real, small black eye gleam. Then his four-foot spar fin rose and sank, the great fluked tail followed . . . and they were gone, leaving the cliffs echoing with the commotion. The Indians believed that if you saw a killer's real eye, you died. It seems quite probable.

John recovered first. "I could easily have shot them, if I'd been closer," he cried, grabbing his bow and arrow.

Nobody else would have wanted to be any closer. Some tribes believe that if you shoot at a killer, sooner or later the killer will get you — inland, or wherever you flee. Other tribes hail him as their animal ancestor and friend, and use him as their crest. But we were not quite sure of ourselves yet — we were just feeling our way along. Perhaps in some former life we had belonged to one of these tribes. But to which one? We had forgotten, but perhaps the killer hadn't. We would take no chances in this forgotten land.

Once more we went our peaceful way, our lines over in hopes of a fish for supper. The engine was barely running — our wake was as gentle as a canoe's. We rounded a bluff and there, on a rocky point, a shaggy grey wolf lay watching her cubs tumbling on the grass. She rose to her feet, eyed us for a second, nosed the cubs — and they were gone.

The distant hills turned violet, then purple. We anchored in a small sheltered cove, made our fire on the shingle beach and ate our supper. Then, all too soon, the night closed in.

About ten the next morning, away off in the distance, we sighted the white-shell beach. A white-shell beach is a distinguished feature of the old Indian villages, and every old village has one. Its whiteness is not a sign of good housekeeping but rather the reverse. These Indians in the old days lived chiefly on seafoods — among them, clams. For hundreds of years they have eaten the clams and tossed the shells over their shoulders. The result is that the old villages, which are believed to be the third successive ones to be built on the same sites, are all perched high up on ancient middens. Earth, grass, fern and stinging-nettle have covered them and made them green, but down by the sea the sun and waves bleach and scour the shell to a dazzling white. The beach is the threshold of an Indian village — the place of greeting and parting.

We dropped anchor between a small island and a great rugged cliff topped with moss-laden firs that bounded one end of the beach. Then we piled into the dinghy and rowed ashore. The place was deserted — for it is a winter village, and every summer the tribe goes off for the fishing. So, when we landed, no chief came down with greetings, no one sang the song of welcome, only a great black wooden figure, standing waist high in the nettles up on the bank, welcomed us with outstretched arms.

"Is she calling us?" asked John, anxiously, shrinking closer to me.

I looked at the huge figure with the fallen breasts, the pursed-out lips, the greedy arms. It was Dsonoqua, of Indian folklore, who runs whistling through the woods, calling to the little Indian children so that she can catch them and carry them off in her basket to devour them.

"No, no! Not us," I assured him. But he kept a watchful eye on her until he was well out of grabbing distance.

Behind the black woman, high up on the midden, sprawled thirteen or fourteen of the old community houses. The same houses stood there when Cook and Vancouver visited the coast. When Columbus discovered America, another group of buildings stood on the same site — only the midden was lower. Now there are shacks huddled in the foreground — the remaining members of the tribe live in them, white men's way. But they didn't seem to matter. One was hardly conscious of them — it was the old community houses that dominated the scene.

Timidly, we mounted the high wooden steps that led from the beach up towards the village platform. It was impossible to move anywhere without first beating down with sticks the stinging-nettle that grew waist high throughout the whole village. In the old days the tribe would harvest it in the fall for its long fibres, from which they made nets for fishing. We beat . . . beat . . . beat . . . and rubbed our bare legs.

The village platform made better walking — a great broad stretch of hand-hewn planks that ran the full length of the village in front of the old houses. We tiptoed, as intruders should. A hot sun blazed overhead. The whole village shimmered. Two serpents, carved ends of beams, thrust their heads out beneath a roof above our heads and waited silently. Waited for what? We didn't know, but they were waiting. I glanced over my left shoulder and caught the cold eye of a great wooden raven. But perhaps I was mistaken; for as long as I watched him he stared straight ahead, seemingly indifferent.

No one knows definitely where these coast Indians came from. In appearance, language and customs they are quite different from the Indians of eastern Canada. They have broad, flat faces and wide heads. There is evidence that in earlier times there was another type with narrow heads and faces — but they have disappeared or merged with the others. There are as many different languages on the coast as there are tribes — each of them distinct and different from any of the others, and with no common roots; and all of them different from any other known language.

Unlike the eastern Indians who elected their chiefs for bravery, the coast Indians had a rigid class system. First the nobility, the smallest class and strictly hereditary; then a large middle class; and then the slaves, who were usually captives from other tribes, and their descendants.

Some ethnologists think that these Indians came across from Asia by the Behring Sea, and worked their way southwards. The Chukchi, who were the aborigines of Kamchatka, used to tell their Russian masters that the people across the straits were people like themselves. Other ethnologists think that they have drifted north from some tropical island of the Pacific. Many of their customs and superstitions are the same. Some customs, whose origin they have forgotten, are similar to those practised by the Polynesians in their old sun-worship.

But whatever their origin, when discovered they were a long way back on the road that all civilizations have travelled — being a simple stone-aged people, fighting nature with stone-age tools and thoughts. In one hundred and fifty years we have hustled them down a long, long road. On a recent Indian grave on a burial island I saw a cooking pot and a rusted boat engine — the owner would need them in the next world. They hang on to the old life with the left hand, and clutch the new life with the right.

The Indians of the interior called the coast Indians "the people-who-live-in-big-houses." The big house at the end of the village street had lost its roof and walls — only the skeleton remained. Its main uprights or house posts were two great wooden ravens with outstretched wings. Fourteen feet high, wing tip touching wing tip, great beaks and fierce eyes, they stared across to where, some sixty feet away, a couple of killer whales standing on their tails formed a companion pair of posts. A massive cedar log connected each pair across the tops of their heads. At right angles on top of these again, enormous cedar logs ninety feet long and three feet in diameter, all fluted lengthwise like Greek pillars, stretched from one pair to the other, forming with the house posts the main skeleton of the house.

The Nimkish tribe have a legend that it was the Raven, he who made the first man, who showed them how to get the huge roof-beams in place. It was certainly the first thing we wondered about. When a chief built his house it was a custom for him to kill four of his slaves and bury one under each house post as it was raised — for strength, or good luck, or perhaps prestige. They had a curious habit of destroying their property just to show how great they were.

The house posts tell to which crest the related inmates of the house belong. The crest system runs through all the coast tribes, even among tribes that have a different language and no friendly intercourse. There is the crest of the Raven, of the Grizzly Bear, of the Wolf and others. The reason why each one is related to, or is the ancestor of, a particular family or clan is woven into their

49

folklore. For instance, there is a legend that the killer whale was created a long time after the other animals. He was made by an Indian, whittled out of yellow cedar. The Indian painted him Indian fashion with an extra eye on his stomach; tried him to see if he would float. Then the Indian told him to go and look for food — he might eat anything he found in the water, but he must never touch man. Unfortunately the killer made a mistake. Two Indians were upset out of their canoe and the killer ate them. Ever since then the killer whale has been related to the family of the men he ate and has been used as their crest.

Beat . . . beat . . . beat . . . we laid the nettles low. A cicada shrilled in the midday heat. And somewhere in the tall pines that backed the village a northern raven muttered under its breath. We lifted the long bar from the great door of a community house, and stood hesitating to enter. In the old days a chief would have greeted us when we stepped inside — a sea otter robe over his shoulder, his head sprinkled with white bird down, the peace sign. He would have led us across the upper platform between the house posts, down the steps into the centre well of the house. Then he would have sung us a little song to let us know that we were welcome, while the women around the open fires beat out the rhythm with their sticks. The earth floor would have been covered with clean sand in our honour and cedar-bark mats hastily spread for our sitting. Slaves would have brought us food — perhaps roe nicely rotted and soaked in fish oil, or perhaps with berries. The house would have been crowded with people — men, women, children, and slaves. Three or four fires would have been burning on the earth floor and the house would have been smoky but dry.

We stepped inside and shivered — the house felt cold and damp after the heat outside. Mounds of dead ashes, damp and green, showed where fires had been. A great bumpy toad hopped slowly across the dirt floor. And one of the house posts — a wolf carved in full relief with its head and shoulders turned, snarled an angry welcome. The only light came from the open door behind us and from the smoke-holes in the roof. High above us, resting on the house posts, stretched the two fluted beams that served as ridge poles. From them long boards, hand-split like shakes, sloped down to the outer wall plates. The walls were covered with the same. Standing in the centre of the house we were about three feet below the outside ground level, for warmth in winter, I imagine. The sleeping platform was on the lower level and ran round the entire house; and behind it, three feet higher, was the platform on which they kept their possessions. In the early days each family would have had a certain space on the two platforms allotted to it, partitioned off with hanging mats. It was a collection of related but separate families, under a common roof. But it was not community living. In that land of winter rains and fog it seems a natural solution to the problem of trying to keep dry. In the summer, as they still do, they left the winter village and went off in their dugouts up the rivers and inlets.

Sunlight and darkness; heat and cold; in and out we wandered. All the houses were the same size, the same plan, only the house posts distinguished them. Some were without wall boards, some without roof boards — all were slowly rotting, slowly disintegrating, the remains of a stone age slowly dying . . . .

Searching . . . poking . . . digging. We found old horn spoons, wooden spoons, all the same shape. Split a kelp bulb lengthwise, leaving an equal length of split stalk, and you have the shape of the coast Indian spoons. Stone hammers, stone chisels. They might have been used to flute the great beams. And why the flutes? Memories of some half-forgotten art, carried across some forgotten sea? In some of the early work there seems to have been a substitution of wood for stone.

In one of the better preserved houses, evidently still in use, there was a beautifully made dugout turned upside down. The Indians still make these dugouts. They take a cedar log the required length, and by eye alone they adze and shape it — keel, bow, stern. When the outside is finished, they drive in wooden pegs, their length depending on the thickness they want the canoe to be. Then they adze, or burn and chisel out the inside until they work down to the wooden pegs. Then comes the work of shaping the dugout, which at this stage is too narrow and high amidships. They fill it up with water and throw in heated stones until the water boils. The wood is then pliable and easily stretched, and they set in the thwarts — spreading and curving the hull to whatever shape they want. The prows are high and curve forward, the tip often carved. This one had the head of a wolf, ears laid back to the wind.

51

We played with their old boxes-for-the-dead, trying to see if we could fit in. It is astonishing what you can get into in the knee-chest position. The owners of these are not allowed to use them now, tree burial is forbidden. The boxes were of bent cedar work, peculiar to these coast Indians, I think. They are made of single sheets of cedar about half an inch in thickness, cut to shape. On lines, where they want them to bend, they cut V-grooves on the inside and straight cuts on the outside. Then they wet the grooves to make the wood pliable, and bend the box to shape, just as you would a cardboard candy box. The edges are sewn together with small roots through awl holes made in the wood. That is necessary just at the last side. The covers are separate, made of a single piece of heavier cedar; flat except for the front edge which curves up and out. The boxes are bound with twisted cedar-bark rope — in a peculiar fashion that leaves a loop at each corner to hold on the lid. When an Indian was alive he kept his belongings in his box. When he died, his friends, always of another crest, put him in his box and tied it up in a grave tree.

It was so easy to let the imagination run riot in these surroundings. All round me, grey and dim, surged and wavered the ones-of-the-past. I picked up a spearhead; smooth brown stone, ground chisel sharp at the edges — and the men of the tribe crowded close. Naked, blackhaired, their faces daubed with red warpaint, their harsh voices raised in excitement. They were pointing at the beach with their spears — the canoes were ready, they were going on a raid, and they raised their spears and shouted.

"Have you found anything?" called Peter behind me . . . and the fierce crowd quivered, hesitated, and were gone.

"Just a spearhead," I murmured, waving him away . . . but they, the dim ones, would not come back.

It was harder to imagine the women. Perhaps they were shyer. I could only catch glimpses of them; they would never let me get very close. But later, on a sunny knoll on a bluff beyond the village, I surprised a group of the old ones. They were sitting there teasing wool with their crooked old fingers, their grey heads bent as they worked and gossiped — warming their old bones in the last hours of the sun. Then a squirrel scolded above my head; I started, and it was all spoiled. On the knoll where they had sat I picked up a carved affair — on examination, a crude spindle. The village lay below me, already in the shadows. Beyond, to the west, quiet islands lay in the path of the sun. And all around me, perhaps, the old women held their breath until this strange woman had gone. I wondered, as I left, what they would do without the spindle that I carried in my hand.

I was tired of Indian villages for the moment — slightly bewildered by turning over the centuries, like the careless flip of a page. So I turned away and waded through the shallows with the youngsters towards the high rocky point with the tall trees, near where our boat was anchored. It was low tide, and suddenly beside my bare foot, which I was placing carefully to avoid the barnacles, I saw an old Indian bracelet of twisted copper. The children were soon making little darting noises, and in a short time we had found a dozen of them, caught among the seaweed or lying in crevices at the edge of the cliff. Some, like the first, were made of twisted copper; others of brass were worked with diagonal lines, and others had the deep grooves at each end that tell of the number of sons in a family. I knew that they belonged to a period about one hundred and fifty years ago, when they first got copper and brass from the Spaniards. But personal belongings like that would have been buried with their owners. Suddenly I remembered the old tree-burials, and glanced above my head at the great trees that overhung the water. There, sure enough, swaying in the breeze, hung long strands of cedar-bark rope that had once bound a box-of-the-dead to the upper branches.

Our supper on board was punctuated with cries of, "There's another box! I see another!" — the whole, still, dark wood, on top of the cliff below which we were anchored, was a burial wood, each moss-hung tree holding its grim burden against the evening sky.

My youngsters are tough, they slept as usual — deep, quiet sleep. I lay awake, lost somewhere down the centuries. Things that I did not understand were abroad in the night; and I had forgotten, or never knew, what charms I should say or what gods I should invoke for protection against them. There were dull lights in the deserted villages. Lights that shimmered and shifted, disappeared and reappeared. Lights that I knew could not be there. I heard the sound of heavy boards being disturbed . . . who is it that treads the village platform? There was a shuffling and scuffing up among the boxes of bones in the trees. Low voices were calling and muttering. Something very confidential was being discussed up in that dark patch.

"Tch ... tch ... tch!" said a voice in unbelieving tones. It was repeated in all the trees, on all the branches, from all the boxes. Perhaps they couldn't believe that we had taken the bracelets — none of their own people would have touched the things-of-the-dead.

"Tch ... tch ... tch!" evidently somebody was telling them all about it.

"O ... O ... O ... O ... !" came low choruses, from this tree and that tree — perhaps they did believe it now, and were thinking up curses.

Impossible to explain to them that I was trying to save their Past for them — a reproving chorus of "Tch ... tch ... tch!" started up immediately.

"But, really," I insisted.

"O ... O ... O ... O!" reproved the Dead.

Finally, exhausted, I watched the first faint signs of dawn. There was soon a more definite stirring in the trees, and one by one the great northern ravens left their vigils and flew off with a last mutter. The owls winged their way deeper into the forest and at last the woods were quiet — the dead slept. Overhead, an early seagull floated in the grey light, its wings etched in black and white — a peaceful, friendly thing. Then I, too, slept.

We stayed three days in that village; anchored three nights beneath the trees-of-the-dead. After all, if it were the whispers and echoes of the past we wanted — here they were.

But we left on the fourth day on account of a dog — or rather a kind of dog. There is always the same kind of peculiar silence about all these old villages — it is hard to explain unless you have felt it. I say felt, because that describes it best. Just as you have at some time sensed somebody hiding in a dark room — so these unseen presences in an old village hold their breath to watch you pass. After wandering and digging and sketching there for three days, without seeing a sign of anything living except the ravens and owls, a little brown dog suddenly and silently appeared at my feet. There is only one way of getting into the village — from the water by the beach. The forest behind has no trails and is practically impenetrable. Yet, one minute the dog was not, and then, there it was. I blinked several times and looked awkwardly the other way . . . but when I looked back it was still there.

I spoke to it — but not a sound or movement did it make — it was just softly there. I coaxed, but there was no sign that it had heard. I had a feeling that if I tried to touch it, my hand might pass right through.

Finally, with a horrible prickling sensation in my spine, I left it and went down to the beach. As I reached the dinghy, I glanced over my shoulder to where I had left the dog — it was gone! But as I turned to undo the rope — it was on the beach beside me. Feeling, I am not sure what — apologetic, I think — I offered it a piece of hard-tack. It immediately began to eat it, and I was feeling decidedly more rational when I suddenly realized that it was making no noise over it. The hard-tack was being swallowed with the same strange silence. Hurriedly, I cast off and left. I didn't look back — I was afraid it mightn't be there.

Later in the morning I said to John — John had been waiting for me in the dinghy at the time —

"John, about that dog . . . ."

"What dog?" interrupted John, busy with a fish-hook.

"That little brown dog that was on the beach."

"Oh, that!" said John, still very busy. "That wasn't a usual dog."

I left it at that — that was what I had wanted to know.

Northward to Seymour Inlet

 HE END OF JULY, WE ANCHORED OVERNIGHT JUST INSIDE the western entrance of Well's Pass, in Kingcome Inlet. We wanted to make an early morning run up the open coast to Seymour Inlet. The entrance to Seymour Inlet is just south of Cape Caution, and that would be the farthest north we had ever been.

We had crept into Kingcome Inlet two days before in heavy fog — soft, white, insistent fog that shut out all our known world. Our once friendly trees were now menacing shadows that would drift suddenly into sight, hesitate for a moment, then swiftly turn and flee away. Instead of clear green sea with its colourful, inhabited shallows, there was a misty void, over which we silently moved. Everything took on the unreal silence of a spirit world. Voices that were thrown with more than usual force were caught and divided and muted, reaching us like soft echoes. We were in the world of the little brown dog, and there was no way out.

Northward we slowly faltered, content if we sometimes saw the ghosts of trees to show that we had not gone too far west and strayed out into the open Pacific. Once something loomed up dead ahead — shrouded in swirling fog — one of the great wooden ravens from the Indian village, towering above us with out-stretched wings? We cowered miserably below him, as I swung the wheel to avoid him. Did he want the bracelets back, or what? He could have them . . . anything! But the huge figure shrank . . . shrank . . . and it was only a lone cormorant sitting on a rock, its wings spread out to dry — magnified by the fog.

Peter had made his own compass — the carving knife, sus-pended on a string.

"Too far to port," he would sing out. "Too far to port."

Every once in a while the knife would swing a full ninety degrees each way. He put that down to something he called "searching." Jan was watching the chart, just in case we saw anything to identify. I couldn't take my eyes off our immediate bow and its perils.

"Everybody's doing something but me," said John, disconso-lately. "What can I do?"

"You could sound for echoes," I said, explaining how the captains of the coast ships in fog blow the whistle in narrow passes or inlets. By counting the number of seconds that it takes a blast to reach the cliff and come back they can work out the distance they are from the cliff. Radar sounds so dull after that. I took my precious whistle out of my pocket and looped it around John's neck.

"It must be a big blast," I explained, "or it won't bounce back properly."

He gathered up all the breath he had in his body — and a mighty blast fared forth into the void. We were all poised to count the seconds — but we had hardly started before back it bounced. I was shattered . . . . I hastily kicked the engine into neutral, for it had bounced from dead ahead. I told John to blow again. Again he threw it out — shrill and piercing — and again it hit and bounced back, undoubtedly from straight ahead.

We inched our way towards it — now ahead, now neutral. I estimated it as perhaps fifty feet . . . . I hung out on one side, Jan on the other. I glanced at the compass to check our direction — we simply must find out where we were and hole up in some place for the night. This fog was not likely to clear unless the wind came up. Jan and I both shouted at the same instant. I stamped the engine into reverse to kill her way. There, ten feet ahead, a straight wall of rock rose out of the sea. I stepped out on the after-deck to get a better look.

"It's all above us too," called Jan from the forward deck.

It was — it rose straight up out of sight.

It was the sea-pigeons that gave us the clue. "It's full of birds," cried Peter. "Sea-pigeons," called Jan. "And cormorants," added John. "One cormorant," corrected Peter.

The fog thinned for a moment, and high up on the cliff we could see ledges and holes in the rocks. Agitated sea-pigeons and the odd cormorant were poking their heads out of the holes, or teetering on the ledges; peering below at the danger that had suddenly loomed up out of the fog.

"Why, its Deep Sea Bluff!" I practically shouted. I hadn't realized we were so far north.

The fog changed its mind and closed in again — blotting out the ledges and the holes. But we had seen the sea-pigeons — it was all we needed. We were just outside Simoom Sound, which is at the entrance to Kingcome Inlet proper. In Simoom, which means "Place of the Winds," there was a logging camp that had been there for twenty-five years. We knew the people who owned it and had tied up there several times before. I got out the chart and worked out the direction from Deep Sea Bluff to the entrance to Simoom.

"Hit on the nose," commented Peter, rolling up his knife and string compass, as the floats and houses loomed up out of the fog.

As is quite usual on the coast, this small logging company was built on a series of huge log-rafts, planked over like wharf floats and connected with gangways. There were comfortable houses for

57

the married men; bunkhouses for the bachelors; cookhouse, work-shop and storehouse. Also bathhouse with stove and boiler and hot showers. And a school. If they didn't have enough children of their own to rate a government teacher, they would board other isolated children for the school year. The teacher came and lived on the rafts with the owner's family.

Two small children dressed in life preservers ran out and stared at us. Then the owner's wife came down to greet us — scold us for wandering around in the fog — ask us up for supper, and offer us the use of the bathhouse and washtubs. We accepted every-thing. Then we tied a lifebelt on John and wandered around the floats, to admire all the flowers growing in tubs or window boxes, to look at the hens and baby chickens in a wire enclosure on one of the floats.

In the evening, when they heard our plans, the loggers told us that there was a deep water passage inside the reefs and kelp as far up as Blunden Harbour — if not farther. They said that the Indians from up there seemed to use it all the time — with their gas boats as well as their dugouts. Our charts showed nothing. They never do when they are used only by Indian dugouts, or us.

"Watch the weather, though," the loggers said. "You don't want to get caught in there with a gas boat if it blows."

The fog was still thick the next morning, so we stayed over and took advantage of the bathhouse, and washed ourselves and our clothes. The fog cleared in the afternoon, and we said good-bye and ran over to Well's Pass, anchoring behind an island just inside. That must have been the island where Captain Vancouver anchored the *Discovery* and the *Chatham* before he went farther north. Both ships went aground in Queen Charlotte Sound the next day.

I woke at about four-thirty and poked my head out of the curtain. The deck was wet with dew — which should mean a fine day. A mother merganser with her brood suddenly caught sight of me. In horror, she turned and fled, her crest streaming out behind her like red hair, her brood paddling desperately after her — on the surface, as though it were mud or snow. A kingfisher started shouting at another one to keep off his territory or he'd split him in two . . . . It was time I was up.

Jan, in the bow bunk, was still asleep. I would leave her for awhile — we could have breakfast later when we got near Blunden Harbour. Young Peter was scrambling into his clothes. He loved to be mate when no one else was around. I started the engine, pulled up the anchor, and nosed out into the Pacific.

It was almost high tide now. It ebbed north here, and we would have the tide with us most of the morning. We kept the main shore in sight. Over to the south-west, where we should have been able to see the north end of Vancouver Island, it was misty and we could see nothing.

The sea was perfectly calm, not a ripple. But when we rounded the last cape at the outer north point of Well's Pass we struck our first Pacific swells. They were wide apart and perfectly gentle. But up we gradually rose . . . and down we gradually sank . . . . Up again . . . down again . . . . A wondering head poked up through the hatchway and made descriptive motions with its hands.

"Where are we?" demanded John, from his bunk. "Why is the sea so funny?"

"It isn't the sea," explained Peter loftily, "it's the ocean. It's been doing it for ages."

The swells had an entirely different feel about them than the waves. Not dangerous exactly, but relentless — an all-the-way-from-China kind of feeling about them. Whatever the sea was doing, I felt that I should like to locate that inner passage as soon as possible. There were cliffs at the moment, so it probably started farther along. I didn't care for the unexpected breaking and spouting of the breakers on a calm surface — breaking on something we couldn't see. We rounded another cape with a great mass of kelp off it. Then I made out a line of kelp extending along the coast as far as the eye could see. From where we were it looked much too narrow to be the Indian passage. Jan went up on the bow, and I worked in closer. It began to look wider and there was evidently a reef underneath or alongside the kelp. Then we came to a gap with no kelp and evidently no reef — nothing that would bother us anyway. We slipped through on top of a swell . . . and here certainly was the Indian channel. It seemed deep right up to the shore, and about thirty feet wide. What low water would show we couldn't tell. There might be no room for the boat at all — the Indians might only use it at high tide . . . . At least the wide kelp bed broke up the swell and none was breaking on the shore.

This was no dash we were making — it was a crawl. There would be no help in these waters if we ran on a reef. We had a good dinghy, but how humiliating to have to row away from our wrecked boat, with no one to blame but ourselves! The tide was dropping rapidly, still helping us on our way. The reef outside of us was now above water in many places; but that only made our channel more secure. The shore, as we had hoped, shelved very steeply. Evidently we were not going to be squeezed between. Around eight o'clock we came to a small group of islands — the Raynor group. Tucking in behind them out of the swell we had our breakfast. We landed on shore for a run, and found our bodies strangely unstable and hard to adapt to the solidness of the rock.

We knew that there was an Indian village in Blunden Harbour and were very tempted. But it would have been foolish not to take advantage of this sunny, quiet day for the run up to Seymour. We passed the entrance to Blunden Harbour — all necks craning. There was no sign of any habitation. So the Indian village must be farther in round the bluff. The entrance seemed quite exposed.

It was lunch time when we pushed thankfully into the South-gate Islands — the end of the open run. We hadn't had any wind at all, but the rollers were distinctly alarming at times. Very frightening when they suddenly broke right ahead of you on a completely hidden rock. They would throw a mass of spray high into the air. The reef would show for a moment in the hollow, and it wasn't hard to see what would have happened to our boat if we had been there.

The loggers at Simoom had told us that the tugs towing log booms were often held up for as long as two weeks in the Southgates by wind. They would have picked up the booms in Belize or Seymour Inlets and come down with the tide to these islands to wait for favourable weather to make Well's Pass. That is the farthest north from which they would try to bring booms. Above there, they would make up Davis rafts — great mounds of logs all tied and wound together with heavy steel cable. Like an iceberg they were mostly below water, and waves and rollers could not wash out the logs — the way they can in a boom.

This circle of the Southgates completely protected the enclosed water and made a perfect booming ground. And it was deep right up to the steep sandstone shores. Cables tied round trees were lying across the slopes, ready for the booms that would come.

The names of various tugs, and the dates, were painted in red or white on the low cliffs. Under some of the shallow caves and overhanging ledges in the sandstone we found oil-paintings, on wood, of various tugs. Amateurish, but some of them quite good. Two weeks is a long time to wait for wind to go down.

The tide was very low now, and we fooled around in the shallows looking for abalones. I can never quite bring myself to the point of eating an abalone. These virile animals, which the Norwegian fishermen tell us should be beaten with a stick before cooking, probably taste like beef-steak with a fishy flavour.

Then, calls from the children to come and see. Up on a dry, grassy point they had found dozens of the abalone shells of all sizes — cleaned out by the seagulls. They nested them together in high stacks. Trading was brisk. Then the air was filled with their unspoken longings. I ignored it — swirling around me, beating about my head . . . then I gave in, "All right," I said, "but down the bilge." If I allowed *everything* they found, on board, there would be no room for us.

We had a swim off the smooth rocks. Lay in the sun to get warm and dry. Then started up the engine and wandered on up to Allison Harbour. We had been told that we might get gas there, and somebody else said he thought there was a store. There was neither. There was a float, and a cabin up on the bank. From the sign nailed up on the wall, it was evidently where the fishing inspector for the district lived. His boat, a heavily-built forty-footer with a high bow, was tied up at one end of the float. He came out on deck when he heard us — then came over and sat on the wharf with us.

When we said we were going into Seymour he told us that he had spent most of the last night caught in the Nakwakto Rapids in the narrow entrance. He explained that you are only supposed to go through at slack water — and the slack lasts only six minutes. He had been twenty minutes late, but thought he could still make it as the tide would be with him. He had barely got started before he knew that he should never have tried it. The current caught his stern and swung him round and rushed his boat against the shelving cliff. That was the end of his propeller. For the rest of the night the rapids that run sixteen knots had played with him. They would rush him along in a back current, swing him out into the through current — then rush him sideways. Then his bow would hit with a splintering crash against the cliff — and the back current would catch him again. Again and again he hit the cliff, and as the tide fell and the contour of the cliff changed, each time he hit in a different part of the stern or bow. Soon he had to pump steadily, three hours of it, as she began to take water. Then, just before slack, when the strength of the current let up and the back currents were not so fierce, Nakwakto Rapids had let go of him. He drifted out of the narrow entrance into Schooner Passage, got out his dinghy and towed his boat into a cove just round the point to the south — a little bay with a shelving beach and an empty Indian shack. He had beached the boat, bow first, which was where the worst damage was, to keep her from sinking, made a hot drink and fallen into his bunk. He hadn't wakened until the sun was high.

A fish-boat had come through Schooner Passage and he had hailed him. They had patched up the bow a bit, and the fellow had towed him back to Allison Harbour.

He showed us the splintered bow — a major job to be repaired. The stern was almost as bad, not to mention the propeller. Plainly, he himself was badly shaken. He strongly advised us to keep away from the place. Finally, he suggested that we spend the night at his wharf, and go up next morning to the little cove with the shelving beach and the Indian shack. There, if we climbed the steep mound to the side of the shack, we would overlook the rapids. We could watch for a while and see what we would be up against. Then we could go through with the flood at lunch time.

"You'll see the little island in the middle that splits the flood tide in two with its pointed bow — a great wave to either side. The fellows tell me that if you stay on it for a tide, the whole rock shakes and trembles with the force of the waters. Turret Rock, they call it. But don't forget, slack only lasts six minutes," he warned.

The next morning found us lying on top of the high mound above the rapids, watching that fearsome roaring hole in action. Turret Rock was not breasting the current, but bracing itself against it on its tail. It was hard to tell whether our mound was trembling, or the island was trembling, or if it was just the motion of the rushing water. Probably the air was in motion from so much turbulence. I am supposed to look calm and collected at such moments, and my crew watch me furtively to see that all is well. I was busy, furtively arguing with myself. It was stupid lying here, holding onto the ground, working ourselves up into a panic. We were used to all the other narrows on the coast — Yuculta, Surge, Seymour, Hole-in-the-Wall. They were all fearsome, and how flat they were at slack! Six minutes slack, I told myself, is not much worse than twelve minutes. In all the other narrows you don't worry about twenty minutes either side of slack. We would be going in on the flood. If all went well we could get past Turret Rock in six minutes. We always tow our dinghy — even if the engine stopped we could tow the boat past the island in ten minutes and then we would be through the worst. The fishing inspector had been in the dark, and he had lost his propeller at the first hit. Looking at the cliffs below I thought there might be fewer back currents on the flood tide — always supposing you got past the island. If we hadn't met the inspector I wouldn't be thinking any of this.

"Come along, youngsters," I said. "Let's get lunch over, and get things ready."

"Are we really going?" they asked, as they slid down.

"When it's dead flat," I said.

I left them on the beach and went back to the boat to get an early lunch ready — preparing for the six minutes. While waiting for the kettle to boil I cleaned the sparkplugs and checked the gaps. Then I cleaned the points on the magneto. Then I wished I hadn't touched anything. Far better to leave an engine alone if it is running well. What possessed me to touch it?

Then I called the children out for lunch. I snapped at every-body. Then someone raised the question whether our decrepit-looking clock was right. I hadn't the faintest idea. We usually judged time by the sun. How could anyone judge slack water in a roaring hole by the sun? I should have to go up on top of the mound and watch it. I pulled up all but the last few feet of the anchor rope, then rowed ashore, leaving a worried-looking crew behind me. I started whistling to cheer them up. Usually, if I whistle, they know that there is nothing to worry about. It was hard to keep in tune . . . a silly, whistling woman, climbing up a mound . . . whistling out of tune.

I watched . . . . I saw the current hesitating . . . . I threw myself down the mound, I rowed breathlessly to the boat. I tossed the painter to somebody and told them to tie her close. I pulled up the crank. The engine started first pull. I tried to swallow — for some reason I was breathless. I yanked up the anchor, and worked out the bay — stood well out, in case we were pulled in . . . .

There was nothing there to pull us in. A still passage lay ahead of us. Turret Rock stood in the middle, looking perfectly quiet and relaxed. We went gently through, resisting the temptation to speed up. The channel opened out into a comparatively wide section. Then the swirls began to form around us — the six minutes must be up. But we were through. I only speeded up because I didn't know where those treacherous back currents might start. How stupid it had all been! Just because we had seen a smashed-up boat, and heard a first-hand account from a worn-out man who had had a bad experience.

Peter shook his head sagely, "You were scared, too, weren't you, Mummy?"

I winked at him. "Weren't we sillies!" I said.

The day had turned out dull and grey and the clouds had settled lower and lower. Whenever I think of Seymour Inlet, I think of it as being low and flat and uninteresting. It is really made up of a series of very narrow, very deep inlets running north-east. These are separated by narrow ridges of high mountains. The whole inlet must be spectacular, if you can see it. I was never sure whether we turned up Nugent Sound and spent the night there, or were at the beginning of Seymour Arm. The first is a blind arm that runs in about eleven miles — while Seymour runs in for twenty-five miles, and ends at a river on which is the winter village of the Wawatle Indians. Nugent and Seymour are separated by a great rib of high mountains — to us it all appeared as low hills.

We spotted a white-shell beach in a short time, so we pulled in near the beach and anchored. There should be a stream; and there was. There was a high mound on the north of the beach which thrust out into the sea. From the top of the mound, on a clear day, you could probably see for miles both up and down the inlet. We had settled on its being the lookout point for the village, which probably lay back of the shell beach — when John fell into the

64

excavation of what had once been a community house. It didn't take long to find the remains of the house posts, which had formed the doorway and supported the roof beams. All very old . . . . How much better to live up on a mound like that, where you could spot the enemy dugout a long way off.

"They probably sneaked up in the fog," said Peter, spotting a weak point.

We found a few slate spearheads, made of slate with a bevelled edge. Farther down the coast they are usually made of chipped flint. The clouds began to drip now, and we went back on board. I took a line and sounded round in a circle. There seemed to be plenty of water if we didn't swing. I carried out a stern-anchor in the dinghy, as we might as well stay here for the night. The *Coast Pilot* had been very discouraging about anchorages of any kind — there just were none, according to them. Well, well! It didn't mention the Indian passage either.

We stuck it out for two more days. It wasn't a downpour, it was just a very wet drizzle, and with no visibility at all. With the canvas curtains closed, and the Coleman stove going, we could keep warm and dry. I had some sourdough on board, which old Mike had given us. So I made bread buns in the iron frying pan covered with a plate. Then we made a pail of baked beans. Usually, we bury the pail in the ashes of our bonfire at night — leaving them there all night. The ones cooked quickly are not as good. But with the beans, and the smell of the fresh bread, we were fairly drooling by the time they were ready to eat.

Then we had the worry of getting out through the rapids again. Still not sure of our clock, we waited around in the swirls at a good safe distance until they quietened down. Then we judged that that must be the beginning of the ebb. We were perhaps a few minutes late but had no trouble.

It had been a long, slow trip down the Indian passage in the fog and rain to Blunden Harbour. Never quite sure where we were. Always the possible wind to worry about. It would be very easy to miss the entrance. Then, in a kindly way that fog sometimes has, it lifted long enough for us to identify a headland and the Raynor group. A few minutes later we slipped inside the entrance to Blunden Harbour.

The chart showed a store and post office. We worked our way across to where it was marked on the right of the entrance. A half-sunken float came out of the fog. We tied up to the least sunk end of it. Above the bank was a long, low building, marked store and post office. But the room was caved in, and a rotting verandah sagged off one end of the building. The chart was plainly a little out of date.

After lunch we piled into the dinghy and, in a dreary drizzle, started off in search of the Indian village. We found it after some time tucked away behind some islands at the north end of the harbour. It looked very small and very dreary.

We landed on the white-shell beach beside a beautifully spiralled pole, on top of which sat a comfortable-looking carved eagle with outstretched wings — looking complacently down on our wet figures. These Indian figures are always so darned indifferent. They take everything, and give absolutely nothing — except that stony silence. Perhaps it was just as well in our case — after a week of almost steady fog and rain, one gentle look and we would all have dissolved in tears.

I diffidently shook the rain from my wet shoulders and followed the youngsters up the steep, hewn steps that led to the village platform. Two community houses stood side by side, with heavily barred doors — and padlocks. Not content with that, a large neatly-written notice proclaimed that "Mr. Potladakami George. This chief of this Nagwadakwa People. It is get away. $265.50." We were plainly not welcome. But we ignored Mr. Potladakami George and his notices and padlocks. We took the-way-of-souls, and entered by the two loose boards, round at the side, that are always left for departing spirits. It was cold inside, and a strong smell of damp earth rose in the darkness. Not exactly inviting . . . but the steady sound of rain on the roof set us to work raking together the bits of charred wood on the place for fires.

A feeble blaze soon flickered, and lighted up the old house with creeping light. The heavy pungent smoke rose and filtered out the smoke hole in the roof, just as smokily as it had two hundred years before. The children crowded closer to me — for as our eyes grew more accustomed to the dim light, the weird carved inmates gradually ventured out of the shadows. The tall, dark house posts took shape; and like some horrible nightmare seemed to grow bigger and bigger — and then showed themselves as great ugly men with hollow cheeks and protruding eyes. The flickering fire gave them movement and expression, and they leered and grimaced and reached at us.

The youngsters were uneasy . . . one by one they made some excuse and scuttled out through the-way-of-souls, and left me.

I glanced to the rear of the house to find the companion-posts, but a great sisciatl, a mythical doubleheaded serpent, lay stretched across a rear platform. In Indian folklore anyone who is unfortunate enough to meet a sisciatl shivers and shakes until his limbs drop off. I was certainly shivering, but I knew it was from the cold. However, I kicked the fire together.

I found the round, dark shapes on the side platforms to be great ceremonial dishes carved out of single blocks of cedar — pairs of animals or birds holding the dish between their outstretched paws or wings. Food was served in these when the chief gave a party or potlatch.

Potlatches are forbidden on the coast now — the authorities think it makes the Indians improvident. I think it probably worked both ways. When a chief gave a blanket potlatch, after two or three days of feasting, he presented each guest with a blanket — perhaps a hundred being given away. After which a very great, very powerful chief sat shivering with not enough to cover him, having given away blankets that had taken him years to collect. But — every guest had to give him a potlatch in return, at some future time. So, in a sense, it was a form of insurance.

In spite of the apparent sophistication of Potladakami George this house had more beautiful carved things than we had seen in any other village. There was a great carved wooden spoon, four feet high, with its bowl as big as a soup tureen. Its handle was an eagle with folded wings, and a human hand supported the bowl. A graceful flying dove was carved of cedar, but when you turned its breast towards you it changed to a hideous man with goggle eyes who stuck his tongue out at you. All rather mixed metaphor it seemed — but Indian folklore is like that.

I picked up a pair of beautifully carved hands, and wondered what they had been used for. But striking them idly together I knew at once.

"Clap . . . clap . . . clap!" At the sound, the whole atmosphere of the old house seemed intensified. In just such a setting they might have been used — smoking fires, steaming clothes, the bang of the wind-lifted roof boards, the splash and drip of the driving rain, and nothing to do on some dark winter evening.

"Clap . . . clap . . . clap!" of the olden wooden hands. Out of the room partitioned off at the rear would have burst the masked Indian dancers, each wearing the mask and pelt of the animal he represented. He of the wolf-mask, see him pick his way along — stepping lightly, slinking, smelling. The bear-mask — lurching clumsily in a near-sighted roll. The finding of the honey. Horrible defeat by bees. Ignominious retreat, tail between legs. Loud laughter of superior wolf and shouts of the delighted audience. "Clap . . . clap . . . clap!" of the wooden hands.

"Mummy!" called a voice, outside the loose boards. "Mummy, are you all right? John is crying."

I pushed my way through the boards.

"Why, John, what is the matter?" I asked.

He wouldn't speak — just clutched me.

"He thought you were probably dead," explained Peter.

John only glared.

"Well, let's get back to the boat," I suggested.

We swung round the bay as we went. Passed close to the burial island. It was very overgrown, but above the nettles and the salmonberry bushes the two heads of a great sisciatl dared us to touch the dead of their tribe.

The rain had stopped before we got back to the boat. I tapped the glass — it was slowly rising. We would leave this village of the Nagwadakwa people in the morning.

Sunday Harbour

 EXT MORNING WE HEADED SOUTH. GREAT HEAVY clouds hung low and white, covering the still-sleeping hills and mountains like a downy comforter. Up we rose on the long swell, and then the smooth hurried slide as it urged us on our way. Peter had the wheel and was managing nicely. Jan and I pulled out the chart and the well worn

Coast Pilot to look for shelter — in case of need, in view of the probable wind.

"What day is it?" asked Jan, looking up from the chart.

Sunday, we finally decided, after much thought and calculation — days get lost or found so easily when you have been playing with years and centuries in old Indian villages.

"Well, here's a Sunday Harbour all ready for us!" I looked over her shoulder — a little ring of islands on the fringe of Queen Charlotte Sound. But sure enough, Sunday Harbour was marked with an anchor as shelter and holding ground. I opened the Pilot book to look it up . . . British Columbia Coast Waters . . . Queen Charlotte Sound . . . Fog Island . . . Dusky Cove. Ah! Sunday Harbour. Pilot book says, "Small but sheltered anchorage on south side of Crib Island. Affords refuge for small boats." I didn't altogether like that word "refuge," it sounded like a last extremity. Still, the name was alluring. So, if we need it, Sunday Harbour let it be.

The nine o'clock wind was now flicking at our heels. The mountains had tossed off their comforters and were sticking up their heads to look about them. It does not take much wind, on top of the swell, to make a nasty sea in the sound. I relieved the mate at the wheel — for it depends on the balance on top of a crest whether you make the long slide down the other side safely or not.

"I don't quite like the mightn'ts!" said John anxiously.

"What mightn'ts?" I asked, as I spun the wheel.

"The mightn'ts be able to swim," said John, eyeing the rough waters that curled at our stern.

But even as we were all about to admit that it was much too rough for our liking, we were out of it — for Sunday Harbour opened its arms and we were received into its quiet sabbatical calm. It was low, low tide — which means in this region a drop of twenty-five feet. Islands, rocks and reefs towered above our quiet lagoon; and only in the tall trees, way up, did the wind sing of the rising storm outside.

Low, low tide — primeval ooze, where all life had its beginning. Usually it is hidden with four or five feet of covering water; but at low, low tide it is all exposed and lies naked and defenseless at your feet. Pale-green sea-anemones, looking like exotic asters, opened soft lips and gratefully engulfed our offerings of mussel meat. Then shameful to say, we fed them on stones, which they promptly spat out. We thought uncomfortably of Mrs. Be-done-by-as-you-did, and wandered on in search of abalones on their pale-pink mottled rocks.

Then, blessing of blessings, out came the sun! Sun, whom we hadn't seen for days and days, soothing us, healing us, blessing us. Sunday Harbour? Yes — but it was named for quiet Christian principles and little white churches; and we were worshipping the old god of the day because he shone on us. Sun, O Sun . . . . We slipped off our clothes and joined the sea-beasts in "the ooze of their pasture grounds."

"Sand-strewn caverns, cool and deep, where the winds are all asleep; where the spent lights quiver and gleam; where the saltweed sways in the stream . . . ." I came up to breathe — Jan and Peter were having a floating competition, Jan was sending up tall spouts of water from her mouth, and the sun was shining on their upturned faces. I looked around for John . . . there he was doing a dead man's float all by himself — face downwards, only his small behind gleaming on the surface.

Somehow, I mistrusted that word "refuge" from the beginning — it was too suggestive of other things, such as trouble or shipwreck. And then one always forgets that Pilot books, even if they say small vessels, probably mean cruisers as opposed to battleships. All day the place was perfect. We might have been in a land-locked lake, miles and miles from the sea. But as daylight faded, the tide rose. And by and by it rose some more — and gone was our quiet lagoon. We could see the wild ocean over the tops of our island, and the waves drove through gaps that we had not even suspected. The wind, which all day had kept to the tree tops, now swooped and tore at our refuge like a wild frenzied thing . . . . And by and by it rose some more — and the gusts of wind swept our little boat in wide dizzying semi-circles — first one way and then the other. I let out more and more rope, but our anchor started to drag . . . and it dragged, and the wind blew, and the tide rose; and finally we were blown out of Sunday Harbour, and backwards into Monday Harbour.

Monday Harbour was another misnomer — a battleship might have held its own, but not a little boat with an uneasy name. I hesitated about staying, then put out two anchors — for the moon was glorious, full and bright; and it swung high, swung low, in the swaying branches. But the wind was making a night of it too. Sleep was impossible with a boat on the prowl; and beauty is only relative. So somewhere in those cold lost hours of a new day I damned the gods of Sun and Moon that led poor sailors from the narrow way, started up my engine and went and found a cove all of my own. Ignored by charts, unsung by *Coast Pilot*, it was calm, it was quiet, it was unnamed. I dropped the anchor . . . and went to sleep.

Morning revealed a white-shell beach in Tuesday Cove. My crew, who had kept no tryst with strange gods in the night, were already swimming when I awoke — their little naked, brown bodies glistening against the shimmering white shell. They are used to waking up in strange coves and accept it without much comment.

"But how did we ever get to this nice place?" I heard John ask.

"We just came, silly!" said Peter. "In the night." His face went under and his feet churned the water to foam.

Karlukwees Village

T WAS DUSK BEFORE WE DROPPED ANCHOR IN KAR-lukwees Bay. It had been slow work feeling our way through the kelp-choked passages, and now it was too late to explore. Dimly above its shell beach the village curved in a half-moon on its high midden. A totem pole thrust itself up into the night. Great shadowy figures, cold and implacable, stared through the grey light at two small islands across the bay. Low white figures were keeping watch over there. One of them looked like a running animal of some kind — sinister, watchful. Burial islands, I guessed unhappily, as the night and the figures crowded close.

The whispering crew soon hushed to sleep. Somewhere behind a tall hill a late moon was hesitating to show itself. But in spite of my foolish tryst with her the night before, in Monday Harbour, I awaited her coming eagerly, for it was dark and lonely with the burial islands and all.

A swift tide thrummed its way through the massed kelp, and the eddies sucked and swirled over some hidden reef. If our boat sank in the night, it might be a couple of months before we were missed.

"That little white boat with the woman and children," somebody would suddenly think. "I haven't seen it around this fall." But by this time the little crabs would be playing in and out our ribs; those horrible figures would still be staring over the water, and we wouldn't be able to tell anybody that we were lying down there below.

We had just started our early breakfast next morning when a great northern raven discovered us and hurried down with welcoming shouts. He perched on a rocky point not far off and inquired about this, that, and the other thing. He chuckled over some of our up-coast news, and regretfully muttered "Tch — tch — tch!" over other bits. Then he proceeded to tell us all the winter gossip of the village as we ate our breakfast. They are the most extraordinary birds. They can ask a question, express sorrow or surprise, with all the intonations of the human voice. The old Indians credit them with unusual powers. A priest told the story of seeing an old Indian sitting smoking on the village beach. A raven alighted on the tree above the old man's head and they carried on a conversation for some minutes — both apparently talking. When the raven flew away the priest went down to the beach and questioned the Indian . . . . The old man was reluctant, but finally said, "Raven say, dead man come to village tonight."

The priest rebuked him for such nonsense — the old Indian shrugged his shoulders and put his pipe back in his mouth. But that night a canoe brought a dead man back to the village.

Our raven was trying to tell us so much that we couldn't understand. Finally, he flew away, "See you again," he unmistakably croaked — and the place seemed empty with his going.

Once more we beat and laid the nettles low. Only one community house was intact in Karlukwees village, but there were remains of at least half a dozen more. Under the spell of the surroundings it was easy to see the old village as it must have been. The house posts in this one house were not carved, but were fluted like the big main beams. Out in front were two fine old carved ravens with outspread wings, standing on the heads of

72

grizzly bears. A thunderbird sat on the edge of the midden and gazed across the bay.

I left Jan trying to sketch the thunderbird, and the other two picking up old blue trading beads; and worked my way through the nettles to a burial tree that I had spotted right back of the village. It was an immense fir, seven or eight hundred years old — so old that nothing could amaze it any more. Streamers of lichen dripped grey from bark and branches. Century after century it had stood there watching the fortunes of the little village at its feet. Had it rejoiced with them in the good times — times of plenty? Wept with them in the bad times — times of battle and famine? Or had it merely held their dead more lightly or more tightly, as required? There were nine or ten boxes still up there, clasped in its gnarled branches. Perhaps the old tree's clutch was growing feeble, or perhaps it was too old to care — for when I stepped round its base to the other side, three blood-stained skulls lay there on the ground. I shrank back in horror . . . but making myself look again, saw that it was only dye off the burial blankets.

After lunch we rowed across to the burial islands. When tree burial was forbidden by the government the natives took to putting their dead on special burial islands, piling up the boxes in small log shelters through which the wind could blow. Each family or crest had its own island. The first one we landed on belonged to the wolf crest — a great running wolf thirty feet long, made of boards and painted white, with red and blue extra eyes and signs, stood guard over the dead of his family. On the other island, a killer whale proclaimed that the dead of his family lay there.

It was important in the Indian mind to be buried properly with carefully-observed rites. People who were drowned at sea could not go to the next world, but were doomed to haunt the beaches for ever. Sometimes they were seen at night shivering and moaning, wandering along at tide level, seaweed in their straggling hair and phosphorus shimmering on their dripping bodies. Poor miserable drowned people . . . .

I decided that I had to leave before nightfall. If anything happened to us in this Land-of-the-Past — and drowning was the most likely — would we have to wander the beaches for ever — moaning and moaning? We were just visitors in this forgotten land — but how could we prove it, or who would believe us?

The sun was setting behind the hills when we left the old village — still so silent, still so indifferent whether we came or went. The thunderbird and the other carved figures still stared across to the islands-of-the-dead, where the last rays of the sun fell on wolf and killer whale. Silent, implacable, it was they who belonged here — we were only intruders; we would tiptoe away.

But as we rounded the last point, escaping, there was a hurried beat of wings, and our friend the northern raven flew croaking out of the dark woods and down to the edge of the cliff.

"What, going?" he chuckled . . . . "Tch — tch — tch!"

The Skull

 T WAS JOHN WHO FOUND THE SKULL, OR RATHER THE bone that led to the skull. He was playing on the beach over in the corner near the waterhole, underneath a great old fir tree that grows on the edge of the bank where the solid rock slopes down lower towards the beach. This old tree doesn't grow tall and straight the way they do in the forest. It sends out huge low branches almost as big as the trunk — as though it were easier to feed its hard won nourishment to the parts not too far away from the source. The great roots that embrace the rocks like an octopus and anchor the old tree to the bank are now exposed on the edge of the beach. The waves of the big winter storms have washed away part of the black earth mixed with shell, leaving the bare roots burrowing down into the sand.

"Mummy!" John called, as I came down onto the beach from the high knoll on the other side of the cove.

"I found a bone." He crawled out from under the roots that framed a little house for him, waving a long, white bone.

Deer leg, probably, I thought, as I walked across to look at it . . . but it was no deer bone.

"I think you have found part of an old Indian."

John dropped it, and wiped his hands on his shorts.

"Where did you find it?"

"In under that big tree."

I took a piece of driftwood and poked about cautiously, close

74

to where he indicated. Whoever it was had been buried before that tree existed. And the tree must be at least three hundred years old — the growth is slow on rock. Then, right up underneath the root crown I uncovered something broad and curved. I worked carefully with my hands, and finally lifted out a yellow skull, which looked at us wanly out of hollow sockets . . . .

It was a flathead, the skull having been purposely deformed in infancy — usually with a board fastened so as to give continual pressure, or a cedar-bark pad while the bone is still soft. This one looked as though it had been bound with something as well, for it had a curious knob on the end. A flathead was a sign of nobility among some of the tribes on this coast, and only the upper class were allowed to deform their babies' heads like that. I think this one had been a woman's — it was too small and delicate for a man's, but judging from the teeth, full grown. Who knows how old it was — the coast Indians didn't usually bury their dead in the ground, but fastened them up in trees.

Just recently archaeologists digging in the big Fraser River midden have found proof (by carbon test, I presume) that Indians lived on this coast eight thousand years ago.

In the last twenty years, on southern Vancouver Island, every now and then someone finds a roughly carved stone head or figure. One, just a couple of years ago, was rescued from a man who was building it into a stone wall he was making. Another was turned up by a plough. I saw that one. It was carved out of coarse rough stone: elongated, pierced ear lobes, and rather Egyptian features. Both the stone and the carving called to mind some of the Toltec carvings in the museum down in Mexico. The present coast Indians don't know anything about them, or who made them.

On examination, the land behind the little bay where we were anchored proved to be all midden — about ten or twelve feet deep. It lay exposed where a winter stream cut through. It was quite a small area, and probably just a summer camp. Across the main big bay, at what we call the Gap, are clam flats. The Indians most likely smoked and dried their clams for winter use, close to where they dug them. I don't suppose they had any ceremonies in connection with the digging of clams — clams being immobile creatures, and not temperamental like the salmon. The salmon were treated with great respect. Once they started running — big schools on their way to the rivers to spawn — no venison must be eaten, lest the fish take offence and go off in another direction. After eating the salmon, the bones were carefully collected and thrown back in the sea — so that the souls of the salmon could return to their own country.

"We're always getting mixed up with Indians and things, aren't we?" said Peter, digging furiously.

"Specially me," said John, holding tight on to his piece of old Indian.

Mamalilaculla

T WAS FAR TOO WINDY TO VENTURE UP KNIGHT INLET that day. After studying the chart we decided to put in the time by wandering through the maze of islands over towards Village Island. There is an old Indian village there, Mamalilaculla, and we had never been in there before. The village was always, at least partly, occupied in summer time; for it had a Church of England mission and a small six-bed hospital for tubercular Indian girls.

The chart marked a cove on the south-west side of the island as Indian Anchorage. Anchorage is always difficult to find in the waters off Knight Inlet. A terrific sweep of wind blows through there from Queen Charlotte Sound, with all the force of the open Pacific behind it. Also, you have tides with a range up to twenty-three feet to contend with.

We found the Indian Anchorage without any trouble — out of sight of the village, and quite a long way from it. We anchored in about three and a half fathoms. The water was not very clear, but I rowed all around and could see no sign of any reefs, or any kelp to mark anything. And after all — it was marked as an anchorage. It was too late to explore further that night. Jan said she had seen the roof of a house or shed in the next bay to the south — but all that would have to wait until morning.

We woke to an embarrassing situation. We found ourselves trapped in a little pool — lucky not to be aground — and surrounded by reefs that we could hardly see over, unless you stood up on deck.

While we were eating our breakfast, feeling very foolish, an old Norwegian appeared on top of one of the reefs and, looking down on us, asked if we were all right. "You won't get out of there for two or three hours," he said. "You anchored too far in."

We gave him a cup of coffee and he helped us free our dinghy, which was balancing on the barnacles. He was in a punt, and we followed him back to where, just round the point to the south, was another bay with his float connected with the shore, and his fish-boat tied up.

He took us up to meet his wife. On the way we passed a frame house — a regular cottage with windows, doors, a verandah and chimney. Just as someone else might have pointed out another house on their property and mentioned casually, "This is our guest house," the old fisherman said, "this is our hen house." It was full of hens — a hundred and fifty White Leghorns occupying a four-room cottage. They all crowded to the screened windows to watch us pass.

"Here comes the missus," he said. I turned . . . down the hill came a stout, grey-haired, elderly woman with an ox-goad in her hand, followed by two oxen pulling a stoneboat with a water barrel on it. When she saw us, she turned and faced the oxen, said something to them and they stopped.

Only they weren't oxen, they were cows. They were heavy, thick-set animals. They looked like small oxen and had rings in their noses. They gave milk, and cream and butter, and worked four hours a day when needed. They hauled the barrel to the well for water, carted all the wood for the winter from the forest, and ploughed and harrowed the garden. I had never seen cows working like this before, but the old man said it was quite usual on the small farms in Norway. They could be worked up to four hours a day without affecting the milk supply.

His wife was very Scottish and full of energy. They had a large garden with all kinds of vegetables and about half an acre of strawberries, protected from the birds with old fish-nets. The strawberries were just ripening, in the beginning of August, almost six weeks later than the south of the province. They had a good market for what they could produce in the summer, as well as eggs and milk all the year round. I wondered where on earth their customers lived in this land of apparently no habitation. There was the Mission, but the rest of the customers lived at distances from fifteen to twenty miles away — in logging camps, or the cannery half-way up Knight Inlet, and the store over in Blackfish Sound. If the customers couldn't get to them, the old man in the fish-boat would deliver to them on his way to the fishing grounds. They always had orders ahead for strawberries.

We lay at their wharf for three days, waiting for the wind to drop. We bought milk and cream, vegetables and eggs; and helped them pick crates of strawberries in return for all we could eat ourselves. This was an unheard of luxury on board our boat. There were various places that we had got to know, over the summers, where we could get fresh vegetables — but strawberries and cream!

One afternoon, one of the missionary ladies walked over the trail from the Indian village and had tea with us. We all sat under the tree, up on the mound overlooking the wharf. She was a most interesting woman, and broadminded. She had been at the village for years, and was in charge of the little hospital. She and her companion were both English — I think the Mission itself was English.

She had many tales — there had been one old woman in the village who was slowly dying. She kept saying, "Me want Maley, me want Maley" over and over again. No one understood what or who it was she wanted. Even the other Indians didn't seem to know. Suddenly this missionary had a brain-wave. She looked through all the old books and magazines she had — until she found a picture of the Virgin Mary. She pasted it on a piece of cardboard and took it over to the old Indian.

"You should have seen that old woman's face, as she whispered 'Hail Mary'," said the Protestant missionary — adding, "I was glad to have made her happy." As far as the Mission knew, there had been no Catholic priests in the district for over eighty years. These Kwakiutl Indians had resisted missionaries and civilization much longer than the other tribes on the coast. The old woman might have been captured from some other tribe.

"But it's discouraging at times," said the missionary. For just when, with the help of the nursing and the religious teaching, they thought they had the feet of the village well on the road to civilization, they would come across something that made them realize that, below the surface, the Indian trails were still well trodden. One winter's day they saw some strange Indians arrive in the village by dugout. Ceremonies were held that night in the big community house. The sounds of long speeches, singing and the rhythmic beating of drums came down the wind — all night. In the morning the strangers left.

Inquiring cautiously, she was told that it was the ceremony of "The paying-of-the-tribute-money." The visitors came from a little village up on big Gilford Island. Once it had been a large village, with a powerful chief. But the Indians of Mamalilaculla, forty years before, had raided it and killed and burned and plundered. They had lost many of their own warriors in the raid, and for that, the little village, which had never recovered, still had to pay tribute or blood-money to their conquerors — the village of Mamalilaculla.

The missionaries had tried to tell the people in the village that it wasn't Christian to keep on exacting tribute all these years. But they could do nothing — the strange Indians still appeared every winter. She didn't know how much they had to pay, or what the tribute was. The old men of the tribe would not talk about it any more. It was a closed book, as far as she was concerned.

She asked us to walk back over the trail to see the village and the mission. It was a lovely walk through the tall hemlock. The path was wide and well trodden; for it led also to the Indian Anchorage, which the Indians used in winter for their fishing boats. All the Indians were away now, only the sick people and the old ones were left behind in the summer time. Captain Vancouver and his officers, in 1792, had never understood all the deserted villages. They thought the people must have been killed off by battle or plagues — whereas they were just following their usual custom of going off for the summer, as they still do. These old villages are their winter villages.

Miss B. said she had done her best to have the young Indian girls learn the ancient arts from the old women of the tribe, but none of them were interested. She took us over to a small house to look at some fabric that an old woman was making. She was the only one left in the tribe who knew how — and the art would die out with her. Miss B. did not know what it was called: she had

79

never seen any like it before.

We didn't see the old Indian working — she was sick that day — but we did see her work . . . . In the Kwakiutl village of Mamalilaculla, on the west coast of British Columbia, this old, old woman of the tribe was making South Sea Island tapa cloth out of cedar roots. The cloth was spread across a heavy wooden table — a wooden mallet lying on top of it.

I am not quite sure how tapa cloth is made. But I believe they soak the roots in something to soften them — lay them in a rough pattern of dark and light roots, and then pound them with a wooden mallet into paper-thin, quite tough cloth.

The early explorers often used to winter in the South Seas, and at times had some of the islanders on board their boats on these coasts. There must be some kind of a connection somewhere. Even the liquid sound of the name of this village, Mamalilaculla, is more like the language of those far away islands than it is of most of the Kwakiutl dialects.

Knight Inlet

T WAS STILL BLOWING TOO HARD FOR US TO START ON the long Knight Inlet trip, but it was time I got my crew back on camp fare. We had all just finished making up my mind that, unless the weather changed, we would go on up to Kingcome Inlet in the morning, when we sighted a ketch working in towards the Indian Anchorage. The old fisherman hurried up onto the bluff and waved them round towards his wharf. The ketch went about, hauled down her sails, then "putted" into the wharf and tied up beside our boat.

We knew the people, and they were going up Knight in the morning. Weather that was too windy for our boat was just perfect for the ketch. Before the evening was over, it was all settled that we should transfer our sleeping bags to the ketch and make the trip together. We could leave our boat tied up just where it was.

We were under way by eight o'clock — with engine. Out by Eliot Pass and Warr Bluff to take advantage of the tide, which would be quite a consideration for the first ten miles or so. The

80

ketch was about thirty-seven feet. With the four youngsters they already had on board, and my three, we were full up but still comfortable.

We had hardly cleared Battle Point when the morning wind caught up with us, and with it some quite unexpected fog — soft and rolling. It would roll down the open channels in great round masses — hesitate for an island, and then roll over it and on. It would fill up all the bays — searching and exploring. It came on board and felt us all over with soft, damp fingers, and we hoisted our sails and fled before it. We escaped before we were very far past Protection Point, and left it rolling up Thompson Sound to see what it could find up there.

Then the sun came up over the mountains, and the wind increased until we were making six or seven knots running before it — quite fast enough if you want to enjoy the surroundings and not give all your attention to the sailing. Soon though, it was impossible to forget the sailing on Knight — which writhes along through the mountains like a prehistoric monster. With every next mountain or valley, the wind took a completely different direction. The big sail would jibe across with a "wha-a-am." We would no sooner get it settled on that side when "wha-a-am" back it would go again.

A little farther on, the wind blew harder, but it was steadier. The mains'l, which had been hauled down, was hoisted again. The mountains grew higher and higher, and gossiped together across our heads. And somewhere down at their feet, on that narrow ribbon of water, our boat with the white sails flew swiftly along, completely dwarfed by its surroundings.

We slopped badly in a beam sea when we turned into Glendale Cove, and some of the crew felt a little squeamish. But we were soon out of it and tied up to a wharf inside a boom-log. We intended to spend the night there, for as far as we knew there would be no other anchorage until we were near the head. A little later, watching the big white combers rolling white and wild up the inlet, we decided that any sailing for pleasure up Knight had better be done in the morning.

There is a salmon cannery in Glendale. While we were there a packer came in with a load of fish. The manager invited us up to watch operations. Most of the operators were Indian women. We watched the fish leap from the packer onto the endless belt, onto the moving tables where the Indian women waited with sharp knives, and then into the tins, in an unbelievably short time. So fast that you still seemed to sense some life in the labelled tins . . . . We rowed up to the little river at the end of the cove, and had some warm fresh-water swimming. There was supposed to be a lake, but we couldn't find the trail.

We left Glendale at five-thirty next morning. As we had hoped, Knight still slept. Great clouds hung low and white, tucking him in like a great downy comforter — and we tiptoed past in the quiet, grey dawn.

Knight Inlet averages about one and a half miles in width. Jervis Inlet about a mile. The mountains are about the same height in each — but Knight gives you an entirely different impression. It is bolder, the reaches are shorter. You no sooner get well started on one reach than a stupendous mountain, sitting on a great cape, shoulders you aside without any apology. You stagger across to the other side, only to be just as rudely shoved back the other way. The mountains in Knight don't just line your way — they block it. Perhaps it was because I was on someone else's boat and not my own, but I have never felt so insignificant, anywhere on the coast, as I did in Knight Inlet.

Then gradually, one by one, the snowy peaks tossed the clouds aside and raised their shining heads to watch us pass, turning, as we did, to show new beauties of some different facet. Then a light breeze drifted up the inlet and made varied patterns on the quiet water. We set our sails, which gradually filled, and helped to carry us gently forward. Long shafts of sunlight crept through the valleys to strike the opposite snow-capped peaks. Down . . . down . . . the shafts slowly dropped and spread . . . then caught and held our white sails. We stretched cold, stiff limbs; the mist rose off our dripping decks and canvas; we shouted, and the sleepy crew streamed up on deck to greet the sun.

We had cups of hot tea to warm us up. Then sat there in the sun, watching reach after reach unfold to reveal something still more lovely. When it became apparent that it was going to be after lunch before we reached Cascade Point, where we were to look for twin waterfalls, we cooked our breakfast and ate it on deck.

The great blocky bulk of Tsukola and Cascade Points thrust

themselves out . . . and out. We were too close to see the six-thou-sand-foot mountain that lay behind. Then just past Cascade Point the Twin Falls leapt into view, divided from each other by a sharp ridge of rock. There was no place there to anchor; but three or four miles farther on, in Glacier Bay, there was a small logging camp. We tied up behind their boom. The children spent the next couple of hours playing in a spur of snow that came right down to the water's edge. Glacier Peaks lie behind the bay — two or three miles inland. I think the spur of snow must be where the old glacier has retreated. Early records mention it as down to the sea. We could have stayed where we were for the night, but when we asked the loggers about possible anchorages, they told us of a place just beyond Grave Point, on the opposite side of the inlet where a valley cuts the mountain. It is marked forty fathoms, no bottom, on the chart; but they told us that, in the left-hand corner, we would find a little beach and creek, with anchorage in ten fathoms.

We found everything just as they had said. That evening we built a great beach fire on the shore of Ahnuhati Valley, and watched the light die off the purple mountains with the white tops on the opposite shore.

We had decided on another early morning run, unwilling to miss the sight of Knight asleep, and Knight awakening . . . . So we left the shores of Ahnuhati Valley and crept out past Transit Point, with Mount Lang and Mount Dunbar white and cold in the sky above us. Then, quite suddenly, we were in glacial water — and we slipped over a sea as dense as milk, which hid all beneath us. Captain Vancouver in his diary speaks again and again of the milky water they encountered at the ends of the inlets. They made many guesses, but never the right one. We slowed down a little . . . gave the capes a little more room. There was nothing else we could do.

Then, still surrounded by the early mists, for it was too soon for the sun to top those sleeping mountains, we slipped into Wahshihlas Bay for breakfast. Afterwards we landed on the wide sand flats to stretch our legs. A rather extraordinary place for sand flats to be. Great rocky Hatchet Point to the north, and Indian Corner to the south. Two miles inland, and centred in the middle of Wahshihlas Bay, Mount Everard rises up in a perfect cone to seven thousand feet — the upper three thousand covered with snow. Although you cannot see it, it is joined by a narrow hog's-back to another peak directly behind it — the same shape and same height. The drainage from that double mountain must sweep the sand out through the bay, and then drop suddenly into those milky depths.

To reach the more solid sand we had to wade through one of those glacial streams — so cold that we were numb to the knees. We raced to get warm, our bare feet sinking into the soft damp sand. Suddenly, beside our footprints, we spied a great webbed footprint . . . Robinson Crusoe-like, we stared — then a great goose, with a loud "honk-honk," flew out of the reeds and flopped down some yards away. We chased it with outstretched hands — again and again it flew and flopped — and again and again we chased it . . . . All at once it dawned on us that we were doing exactly what she wanted us to do — and we ran back to find her brood.

"Honk-honk!" warned the mother goose, and not a gosling stirred.

There was no hurry — it was only ten or twelve miles up to Dutchman's Head, which, as far as that deep-keeled boat was concerned, was the end of the inlet. We could either stay near Dutchman's Head for the night or come back to Wahshihlas Bay to get a good start down the inlet in the morning. We would be bucking wind the whole way down.

When we got well out beyond Hatchet Point we could see the sun shining on the great glaciers that stretched towards the east. The still larger one to the west was obscured by high mountains. We could see nothing much below the surface of the water, and when the lookout in the bow called out "Deadhead!" we had to slow to a crawl. Deadheads are big logs, almost waterlogged, that float straight up and down. Many of them have a couple of feet showing above water, but just as many are floating a foot or so below the surface. They can rip a bottom out, or tear a propeller off. This last reach was full of them; and also with great stumps that floated with their roots all spread out like tentacles.

We "putted" along, barely moving, with four lookouts up in the bow, and gradually worked our way across to Dutchman's Head. It was too deep to anchor, so we tied on to a deadhead that seemed fairly stationary. We were at once attacked by starving deerflies — something like horseflies, but bigger, and grey in colour with pointed wings. You could kill them on your legs at the rate of one a second. We had to eat our lunch below — on deck there was not a chance to get a bite in.

We had a parcel for the people who lived near Dutchman's Head — the only white inhabitants of the region. They had lived there for years and the man was a well-known guide and trapper. So we landed all the youngsters on the flats of Ah-ash-na-ski Valley, then rowed over to the new log cabin. I could see the children racing around waving bunches of reeds — evidently the flies were bad in there too.

The cabin was delightfully dark and cool after the glare and heat outside, and it was well screened. They told us that the flies only lasted six weeks, and were over by the time the hunting season began. But up in the mountains there were no flies anyway, just down in the valley.

The talk turned to hunting, and then naturally to grizzlies, which abounded and promptly killed any other animals they tried to keep. The man offered to put us up a tree later, where we could safely watch them feeding below. No, he had never heard of grizzlies climbing trees, their claws were too long. Every afternoon about four o'clock half a dozen of them and some cubs came down to the flats to catch fish and feed.

"Funny thing," he said, "they never seem to go for women or children — they don't pay any attention to my wife, but as soon as they see me they come straight for me — they don't like men."

"What flats do they come to at four o'clock?" we asked.

He pointed. "Along there, at Ah-ash-na-ski Valley."

We got hurriedly to our feet and looked at watches. It was now almost half-past three. The boys we had left on the flats ranged from fourteen down to five. Just when did a grizzly consider that a boy had reached man's estate? Was four o'clock the same on a sunny day as it was on a dull day? Or did it just depend on when the bears felt four-o'clockish, and simply had to have their tea? Our reactions were simple and to the point . . . we rowed wildly to the rescue, our shouts drowned in the roar of the streams. Not a single child paid any attention to us. I transhipped the others to the ketch to start the engine and follow — the dinghy would not hold everybody.

It wasn't until I ran right up to the children that they heard me; they were busy examining the huge spoor of those same chivalrous grizzlies that never touched women or children, but always made for the men. I explained in a hurry — and we reached the dinghy all at the same time. No one would go back for a line they had left under the tree, and nobody breathed quite properly until we were safely on board the ketch.

We made a hurried tea before we faced the deadheads and the flies. The tracks of the bears grew longer and longer as the children told the story and argued.

"Look! Look!" they shrieked, and we scrambled up on deck after them.

There under the tree on the flat were five big bears — twice the size of black bears — and three small cubs — all smelling the footprints the children had made under the trees ... lifting and swinging their noses high in the air ... trying to trace where the intruders had gone.

"Whose been stepping on *my* sand?" growled John. And all the youngsters took up the cry, and the bears came closer and looked at us.

The trip down Knight was wearing but uneventful as far as Ahnuhati Valley, where we were thankful to creep into the little bay and get out of the wind. Once more our fire at night lighted up the surrounding cliffs and water with its flickering flames. And once more the sense of humility at the feet of the reaching mountains.

We left at six in the morning, hoping to get to Glendale before the worst of the wind got up. It always blows up Knight in the summer, gathered and funnelled in from the open Pacific. But the wind had similar ideas about an early start, and before long our small engine could only push the heavy boat at a poor three knots — pounding into the seas, the spray flying high. Finally we put up the jib and mizzen to steady us, losing time but gaining in comfort. Then the engine sputtered ... and died. There was little or no room to tack, with every shore a lee-shore and no possible anchorage. One of us tried to keep the boat in mid-channel, while we drifted backwards or stood still under the two little fluttering sails. After a long, long time the trouble was diagnosed — and once more we fought our way along.

It was rolling high and white when we reached the more open stretch off Glendale. After struggling ahead for a while to get a better slant, we tacked into the bay under a reefed mainsail. It was three o'clock before a very wet and weary crew lowered the sail and moved in behind the boom.

Once more we left at six o'clock — the wind too. At eight, uncertain of our engine which was acting up, we took shelter behind a log boom which was also taking shelter behind an island. At five o'clock in the evening it began to rain and the wind dropped a little. We started off again hoping to get to Minstrel Island for the night. But at dusk, wet and cold, we thankfully crept into Tsakonu Cove, in behind Protection Point. We anchored and stumbled below to get dry and fed, only to hear a shout that the anchor was dragging.

There were no waves in there — but it was low land behind, leading through to a bay on another channel, and the wind blew through and we dragged right out of the bay. Twice we dragged — the bottom was evidently round stones from the creek at the head. Then we put down the big eighty-pound kedge and got some rest.

It was good to see our own little boat again and to find her safe, but rather smaller than I remembered — Knight would have been a little tough in her.

Fog on the Mountain

 SUPPOSE IT IS THE CONFINED QUARTERS OF A BOAT AND the usually limited amount of standing room on shore that makes the idea of walking or climbing so enticing. Which, being so enticing, makes one completely forget that the same cramped quarters are hardly good training for mountain climbing.

John, for two or three years, was a complete ball and chain. I suppose I must have walked miles with him astride my hip, on more or less level trails. It was the time in between — when he was too heavy for my hip, but not big enough to attempt the longer hikes or climbs, that we were most tied to the beach.

One September we bribed John to stay behind at sea level with some friends, and five of us set off to climb six or seven thousand feet up behind Louisa Inlet. We planned to stay on top over one night, so each of us had to carry a blanket or sleeping bag, plus a share of the provisions. The last we cut to a minimum — tea, as being lighter than coffee; rye-tack lighter than bread; beans, cheese, peanut butter — the least for the most. Even then, half-way up we would all have gladly slept without blankets and starved until we got back. A pack certainly takes the joy and spring out of climbing.

A mile, I believe, is 5,280 feet. If you climb 5,280 feet you are *not* going to be on top of a mountain of that height.

Our first point was a small trapper's cabin at 600 feet. It was at the end of a skid-road that sloped up fairly gradually from sea level. I am sure that it was nine times 600 feet before we sank panting beside the cabin, and it seemed breathlessly hot there, in the middle of the tall trees. We drank from a running stream, we bathed our faces and arms in it, and bathed our feet in it while we emptied the earth and gravel out of our running shoes. "Doc," who led the party because he knew the way to the top and had carried by far the heaviest pack, sat there deploring the idea of our waterlogging ourselves. The man off a yacht, who had come to go half-way with us to take pictures, spoke longingly of lunch. But Doc pointed out that lunchtime and the half-way mark was not until we reached the cliff where the black huckleberry patch was. That we knew perfectly well. We had all been as far as the huckleberry patch — but never with packs on our backs.

We made fresh blazes on some of the trees as we moved on — double blazes at some of the turns. The man off the yacht was going back by himself, and it was not good country to be lost in.

At long last — at 4,000 feet — we climbed the "chimney" and sank exhausted beside the huckleberry patch. We boiled a billy for tea, and ate the sandwiches that the yachtsmen had carried for the first meal. There were not many huckleberries left. A little late in the season, but I thought, judging by the broken branches, that the bears had been feeding on them.

Doc warned the man off the yacht against attempting any short cuts on the way back, there just were none. Then we shouldered our packs, said good-bye to him, and started climbing.

Doc had been up once before, so knew the general direction we had to take. He was looking out for a diagonal stretch of red granite — an intrusion in the midst of the grey granite. If we could find it — and we had to find it — it would lead us up the next two thousand feet. After some false starts, and having to retrace our steps, we spotted a cairn of stones. Doc identified it as the place where we had to begin angling up towards the beginning of what he called "Hasting Street." We could see that if we didn't angle we would get involved with cliffs ahead. Once on Hasting Street we would start angling back in the opposite direction.

It was time for another cup of tea before we finally came out on Hasting Street. We had spent the last couple of hours scrambling up and down and over . . . and up again. Cliffs above us and cliffs not far below us. Then suddenly, in the midst of the tall mountains, we came out on an almost civilized highway — a strip of smooth red granite stretching up at a forty-five degree angle. It was perhaps thirty feet wide, with a gutter of running water over on the left side. The road itself was smooth and dry, with no obstructions. It was the uniformity of its width that was its most arresting feature — after you recovered from the shock of its being there at all.

We drank from the gutter, we bathed our tired feet, we lay down on the hot rock in the sun . . . . All but Peter, who ran up and down, sailed scraps of paper in the gutter, and raced down the smooth granite to intercept them below. The resiliency of small boys always astonishes me — they are either awake and in constant motion or else asleep and unconscious — nothing in between.

The Doc looked at his watch, and remarked that it was still a long way from the top — and it was now almost five o'clock. Far down below, the sun would have left the little inlet. But up here it still shone on our bent backs, and a blast of hot air came up from the rock as we toiled along. The calves of our legs stretched and stretched . . . the soles of our running shoes got hotter and hotter — and we could feel the skin on the soles of our feet cracking and curling. We would stop for any excuse at all . . . and then trudge, trudge again . . . . Doc started zigzagging, and we all followed. That cut the angle in half, but lengthened the distance. However, it did help our laboured breathing.

Then the peaks of the mountains came into sight ahead of us . . . then the snow-filled gullies . . . and our tiredness was forgotten. Towards the west, as far as we could see, there was one vast expanse of snow, dotted with snowy peaks poking through. We were level with it all, and couldn't see the valleys and ravines that must cut down between the peaks. It was easy to imagine putting on skis and gliding across the snowfield the whole way to Desolation Sound. But we knew that quite close on that snowfield it was possible to step off the mile-high cliff and fall straight down to the inlet below. We knew that, if we followed the ridge we were now standing on to the south-east, it would lead us over to Potato Valley and on down in the Queen's Reach of Jervis Inlet. A prospector had told us of trips he had had up on the ridges that skirted the ravines. There were mountain sheep that followed the ridges from valley to valley — hunting the green leaves and grass. And the grizzlies followed — hunting the sheep. He told us of one night, a couple of ridges over from where we were now, when he had barricaded himself in a cave, with his rifle across his knees — and two grizzlies had prowled outside all night, standing up and drumming on their huge chests, the way gorillas do. He hadn't exactly enjoyed that night — then he put his hand in his pocket and pulled out samples of quartz flaked with gold, and pure white quartz crystals that they use in optical instruments — it was for these that he followed the ridges.

The peak above us, on which the summer sun shone all day, was dull, grey granite — but the snow lay about its feet like a slipped garment. Looking west, we were on the north side of all the dozens of peaks over towards Desolation Sound — and the sides towards us were fully clad in white, without any hope of ever melting. The autumn snow must already be falling on them at times.

We had a snowball battle but the snow was coarse and granular and didn't hold together well. The sun left us suddenly, and we were cold and tired. Doc suggested that we find a place for the night and get some food inside us.

It took some time to find a place — among the moss in a more or less level place. We collected little twigs from some kind of scrub mountain plant, to try to get warm. But the twigs didn't have any warmth in them. We were so thankful that Doc had insisted on adding a primus to his load. We heated a couple of tins of beans, and a billy of water for tea. Food made everyone feel warm again.

But a camp is not a camp without a fire. It was getting too dark and cold to do any exploring, so we decided to turn in at once and get up early to do our exploring, and take pictures when the sun first hit the opposite mountains. It would only take half a day to get back to the inlet.

Whatever made us think that one blanket each would keep us warm! Doc had the large eiderdown lining of a sleeping bag. It opened out full — and he and Peter decided to double up — Peter's blanket under them, and the sleeping bag over them. The two girls found a hollow and filled it with moss — then curled up there together, under two blankets. I was left looking at my one blanket. None of us undressed — we put on all we had. But sweaters, shirts and shorts are not very much. Everybody except me seemed to settle down, and the deep breathing of unconsciousness soon rose from the smaller mound.

I got colder and colder . . . . I couldn't feel my feet at all. I made plans. I waited until heavier breathing from underneath the eiderdown sleeping bag indicated that Doc was finally off; then stealthily I crept closer. Cautiously I felt for the edge of the sleeping bag, listening . . . steady deep breathing from Doc. I could count on Peter not to waken — small boys never do. I pushed him over against Doc and crept in, dragging my blanket after me. Oh, the blessed warmth of Peter's small hollow in the moss . . . the blessed heat of his small back! Nobody stirred — nobody dreamt that an iceberg had slipped in to spend the night.

I was wakened in the morning by something dripping on my face. I put a hand out cautiously, thinking that someone was playing a joke . . . but the whole sleeping bag was soaking wet. I opened my eyes — it was lightish, so it must be almost morning . . . but I couldn't see a thing. We were engulfed in a thick, wet blanket of fog — on a mountain-top, a long way from home. Then I heard the sound of the primus being pumped, and I called out to Doc, who certainly wasn't in the sleeping bag — and neither was Peter. Doc's face appeared wreathed in white mist, looking wet and worried; Peter's bursting with excitement — real adventure, lost on a mountain-top.

Doc, I could see, was really worried. Unless we could manage to find Hasting Street, we wouldn't be able to get down off the mountain. We only had enough food for two meals, and no way of keeping warm. We drank the hot tea, warming our hands on the hot mugs, and scrunched a piece of rye-tack. Doc thought it would be better to pack up at once and start down, then eat later. We rolled up the dripping blankets and sleeping bag in long rolls and hung them round our shrinking necks.

Then, hand in hand, not daring to lose contact with each other, we inched along hoping we had come that way when we were looking for a camping spot. We couldn't see a thing; there was nothing familiar underfoot. You could see the person whose hand you held — like some fellow spirit — but not the one beyond. I thought we were probably working too far to the right and towards the peaks — in our fear of bearing too far to the left and the cliffs. How slow were our uncertain feet; so reluctant, yet so eager!

Then, suddenly, out of the mist on the right, Jan called out, "Here is the snow!" and added a second after with a shout. "And here are our footprints!" Doc questioned us closely on whether any of us had walked in the snow after the snowball fight — nobody had, we were sure. Then he said that he knew now just about where Hasting Street was. We would have to risk bearing farther to the left or there would be a danger of passing it. Hanging tight to each other we strung along.

"Here it is, I think!" shouted Doc. We couldn't see him, and his voice sounded all woolly and blanketed.

We crawled up to him and cautiously spread out in a line to the right. There it was . . . we thought. One end of the line searched for and found the gutter, and then we were sure.

We had ideas of a quick walk down the next two thousand feet of altitude in next to no time. Doc was the first to sit down with a bang before we had even started. Then my feet shot ahead of me, and I sat there jarred to the teeth. Dry granite was evidently one thing; wet granite was quite another. It might as well have been ice, to anyone in running shoes. We had to sit and slide or else walk in the stream the whole 2,000 feet — of altitude, not linear feet. It took us over three hours. We still couldn't see more than three or four feet ahead of us — enough perhaps to keep us from stepping over a precipice, but not enough to give us any sense of direction. Then Hasting Street came to an end.

By far the most difficult part was getting from the end of Hasting Street to the place of the rock cairn. Coming up, it had been tough enough, the scrambling up and over and down — cliffs above us and precipices below us. But now we couldn't see where the cliffs were, or how close the drops — it was nerve-racking.

We stopped for ten minutes' rest. Doc broke off a chunk of cheese for each of us to keep us going. As we sat there, on boulders, young Peter picked up a stone and lobbed it into the fog. It disappeared . . . but didn't land . . . . Seconds later, we heard it land a long way below. Peter sat down suddenly and held on. We were not more than ten feet from the edge of that drop. Doc felt fairly sure that we had either missed the cairn, or were within a hundred feet of it. There had been only one sheer drop as deep as the sound of that stone between the cairn and Hasting Street. We tried it again with stones, and counted the seconds until they hit. It still didn't tell us which side of the cairn we were on — but it did tell us that there was a four-hundred-foot drop.

We couldn't leave each other to scout ahead, but we tried to estimate the number of feet we covered now. Also we put stones on top of the rocks so that we could find our way back to the cliff — if we decided that we had already passed the cairn where we should make a turn.

"There it is!" a woolly voice cried. It was six feet to the right. In shrinking away from the cliffs, we had almost over-shot our marker.

The fog thinned momentarily, as though we had done our bit so it would help a little. Doc plunged ahead, with the rest of us like a comet tail behind him, seizing the chance to locate the huckleberry patch. That would mark the chimney we had to climb down towards the trapline with the blazes. Finally there was a shout from Doc — there they were, and there was the chimney. The fog closed down again before we quite got to it. Again we held hands, and advanced cautiously towards where we had spotted it. One by one we took off into space, with the horrible thought that it could be the wrong chimney. We hung on tooth and nail, dislodging stones and earth in our urgency. Another shout from Doc — there was a tree . . . there was a blaze — we were safe.

93

We got out the primus, and while we were waiting for the water to boil we wrung out the sleeping bag and blankets again. We munched bully-beef and rye-tack, and finished up with peanut butter. Then we sank as deep as we could in our mugs of hot tea.

Two thousand perpendicular feet below we came out into bright sunshine. Two thousand feet more and we were back at the wharf. Nobody had been worrying about us at all. It was just another lovely day, down in the inlet. We made our squishing way to the dinghy and back to Trapper's Rock. There we fell into the sea — clothes and all. How warm the water felt, how hot the last rays of the Louisa sun!

We cooked ourselves a great pan of bacon and eggs — a big pot of coffee, and great spoonfuls of honey on top of peanut butter and crackers. Enjoyment is always greatest when you have enough contrast to measure it by.

Speaking of Whales

 HERE DO YOU COME FROM? WHERE ARE YOU GOING? I would wave a vague hand behind me. "Oh, from the south," I would say evasively, or, "Oh, just up north — nowhere in particular."

What did it matter to anyone where we went? We ourselves usually had some idea where we intended to go. But we seldom stuck to our original intentions — we were always being lured off to other channels.

Sometimes that wasn't our fault. One summer we seemed to be beset with whales. Northern waters were a little strange to us then; and so were the particular kind of whale they had up there. We were used to the killer whales, which we often saw in southern British Columbia — they were black with the white oval splash that looked like an eye, and they were white underneath. They also had high spar-fins, sometimes four feet in height. You seldom saw them alone — they went around in packs. They would go charging through the narrow pass at home — blowing and smacking their tails. "Killers in the pass, killers in the pass," the children would shout, from here and there. And everyone would race down to

Little Point to count them through.

The ones we saw up north were grey, or perhaps a dirty white — and very big, twice as long as our boat. They often lazed around on the surface, just awash, and blew huge spurts of air and water up into the air. You would see the spurt, and then have to wait until the noise reached you — something like a pile of bricks falling slowly over — and the sound would echo from cliff to cliff, until it whispered itself out.

They would patrol backwards and forwards . . . backwards and forwards . . . across some inlet we wanted to go up . . . and we would meekly turn back. They didn't appear to be feeding — just pacing the water. Perhaps they were waiting for their babies to be born — which is rather a critical proceeding. For when the baby is born into the water, the mother whale has to put her flipper round it and rush it to the surface to take its first breath, or else it will drown. Then it has to be initiated into the business of nursing. The two nipples are up near the bow of the whale, just behind the head. The nursing is probably, in the beginning anyway, a near-the-surface operation. The baby whale does not exactly suckle. It takes the nipple in its mouth, and the mother ejects a huge supply of milk into the baby in one blow — and that is all for another half-hour, when the procedure is repeated.

That same summer, going back by Johnstone Strait on our way south, we were overtaken by a whole pack of killer whales. We didn't hear them coming — they were just suddenly there, on all sides of us, big ones and little ones — all just playing. There must have been about twenty of them — chasing, diving, ducking and rolling with tremendous slaps of their tails. When you see the spar-fin of a big killer breaking water, it is like seeing the mast of a fishing boat appearing from behind a swell on the skyline.

The biggest of these were around thirty feet, with a fin four or five feet in height. When one of them breaks water the head comes up first; then it submerges and the spar-fin rolls up. Just as the fin disappears, a flange of the tail rolls into sight, looking like another fin, but smaller. Then with a tremendous smack of the tail, the whale submerges.

But this pack were not travelling, they were playing — putting in time. One of the big ones chased or pushed a smaller one straight up in the air, clear of the water; and its chaser followed, out to the shoulders. One of them surged straight for the shore when chased. He hit the shallow water with a force that stood him straight up on his head — a great bleeding gash showing on one side. He fell back and somehow managed to struggle back into deep water. Our fears increased after that. There was nothing to prevent them coming up underneath our boat — quite unintentionally.

But we couldn't escape from them — they were between us and the shore, and on all sides of us. We couldn't hurry, we couldn't lag behind — they either hurried too, or else waited for us. Mile after mile . . . at last, at some unknown signal, they all dived deep at the same moment — and the sea was quiet and empty, and our ears rang in the stillness. When next they surfaced they were heading full speed up a channel which, if they intended to continue south, would take them through the Green Point Rapids.

"Do you suppose they wait for slack water?" said Jan.

"Perhaps that's why they were just fooling around," suggested Peter.

"I didn't like that fooling!" Said John.

I got out the tide book, and looked up the slack water tables. Slack water has not necessarily much to do with the height of the tide. Yes, it was just half an hour before slack water in the Green Points. If they hurried, they could get through the Green Points, the Dent Island, and the Yucultas, all in the same slack. That was evidently just what they intended to do.

I revved up the engine and we chased after them. We couldn't hope to get the whole way through, for it was a big run-in. But we could get through the Green Points, and then cut in behind the Dent Islands and tie up for the night. The fishermen there would tell us what the killers had done.

"Don't go too fast," said John, anxiously.

"Oh, I can't catch up with them," I reassured him. We certainly wouldn't care to be escorted through the rapids by a school of whales.

The killers are savage things. They normally hunt in packs. But once we saw a savage fight between a lone killer and a small grey whale — very one-sided, since the grey whales have no teeth. The killer had chased it into shallow water. They went round and round — in and out among the reefs. The killer must have been taking bites out of the grey one whenever it got close enough — the water round them was foamy and a bright pink. Then the grey one made a break for more open water — the killer hot on its tail.

They turned up a blind channel — so the outcome was not in much doubt.

Another time, near home, I was awakened in the night by the loud tail-smacks and blowing of killers in the pass. I could tell by the direction of the sounds that they must have turned into the bay. The next morning the children came running into the house to report that there was a crowd in the cove on the other side of the bay, all gathered round something on the beach. I took the binoculars over to the point, but I couldn't make out what the crowd were interested in. We piled into the canoe and paddled across.

Most of the crowd had gone by the time we got there. But a group of fishermen were still standing talking beside a small grey whale that lay on its side on the mud. It was still alive. Every now and then it would let out a great gusty sigh. There was a big gash in one side, but not enough to kill it. The fishermen said they had also heard the killers in the night; and later they had heard the commotion in the shallows.

"The whole pack of them went ploughing right past our boats," they said. "Evidently, they had all ganged up on this little fellow, and chased him right in the bay, where he got stranded."

The sun was quite hot, and there wouldn't be enough tide to float the whale until the evening. The men were throwing the odd pail of water over it to keep it damp. But the poor whale sighed, as though it didn't think it would help much. I think they are like porpoises and have no sweat glands — without the water to keep them cool, they over-heat. That night the fishermen put a rope round its tail and towed it a long way out. It was still alive, but they didn't seem to think it would survive.

Our clock is not very reliable — the tide had not quite turned when we reached the Green Points but it had no force left. We played the back currents, and got through quite easily. Another twenty minutes and we could feel the push of the current. Once we passed Phillip's Arms, I struck across over to the north side — the current carrying us almost as fast to the east as we made north. One of my nightmares is having the engine stop just above the rapids. If I didn't get in behind Dent Island we would be swept into the worst of the rapids. A huge whirlpool forms in the centre there, and everything is drawn into it from all sides.

I let out my breath as we edged our way into the bay at the back of Big Dent. We tied the boat up to a boom log and ran across to the other side of the island to watch the big run-in. A couple of fish-boats were lying inside a boom, and we went across to ask them about the whales.

"Did the killer whales go through?" I asked the men.

"Sure, about an hour ago — they always wait for slack water."

But they weren't sure whether they waited because they didn't like the current, or because it was the best time to fish. What we really wanted to know was, how the whales knew when it would be slack water.

We sat on the cliff and watched the whirlpools forming and moving across; then the final hole in the middle, swallowing up the sticks and logs. If you meet a whirlpool, you are supposed to decide calmly which side to take it on — one side throws you out, the other draws you in. I always forget at the critical moment which is which. However, there are many local stories of boats that have been sucked down, or had narrow escapes. One story the people tell is of a small fish-boat whose engine had stopped, and which was going round and round in a whirlpool. An Indian, seeing it from the shore, paddled out in a small dugout and took the man off — just as the boat filled and sank.

In the Arran Rapids, which are on the other side of Stuart Island from the Yucultas, a Catholic priest was being paddled through them by four Indians in a dugout. The priest was terrified when he saw what they were proposing to take him through, and began to pray out loud.

"Don't worry!" the Indians told him. "Our gods will look after us. They always make a straight way for us through the rapids." The priest said later that, in the middle of all that awful turbulence, there was a straight shining path, leading them the whole way through. When they had safely landed him, he fell on his knees to give thanks to God, and explained to the Indians what he was doing.

"Uh!" said the Indians. "We give presents to our gods first."

The Nimkish

T WAS UP NEAR THE NIMKISH RIVER THAT I WHISTLED the little duck to bed. John must have been very small that summer, for I had rowed him out to the boat to put him to bed. Friends had come over from the lumber mill to spend the evening with us round our fire on the beach, and it was going to be too late for such a little fellow. John was full of tears and woe, and threats of what he was going to do if I left him alone out there.

To divert him, I pointed to a little duck that was floating around, all alone at dusk.

"Poor little duck — he hasn't got any mummy to put him to bed."

"I don't care," sniffed John.

"I'll whistle to him, and tell him to come and sleep with you."

I started a low monotonous whistle — two short, one long; two short, one long; over and over again. The lonely little duck started coming slowly over towards us. John sat up to watch.

"Don't talk," I whispered — my low monotonous whistle would have hypnotized anything. But how did the little duck know that it meant "Come to me, come to me?" He came on, right up to the boat. Still whistling, I slowly put my hand down and gently picked him up. He didn't struggle — just kept murmuring his own little monotonous triplet.

I handed him to John, who wasn't at all sure how to manage. He had never slept with a duck before — and the duck didn't like being covered up. John finally sighed and passed him back to me.

"You better keep it," he suggested, and put his thumb in his mouth — the crisis was evidently over.

I put the duck in my blazer pocket and rowed ashore. They had all been watching and everyone was convinced that I had strange powers. None of us was sure just what the little duck was. It was like a sea-pigeon or guillemot, but I don't remember red legs. The youngsters took turns holding it for the rest of the evening. Later they fixed it up in the rowboat for the night. In the morning, much to John's sorrow, the little duck had gone. Jan and Peter drove me nearly crazy for the rest of the summer trying to whistle ducks to bed. I refused to try again — I thought I would rest on my one success.

It was a couple of nights later, coming down below the Nimkish, that the cougar kept prowling around and howling all night. I don't know just where we were and I didn't know at the time. We were coming down Johnstone Strait in dense fog and with no compass. It had been lost overboard — a painful episode, and full of tears; we won't go into it. The straits are only a mile wide. You would think that it would be easy to keep straight, for that short distance, and get across. I tried twice without success. Usually, by watching your wake, you can keep a reasonable course. But we couldn't see our wake for more than a couple of boat lengths.

The last try, we started from a fixed light on a point — it was high and white and conspicuous, which gave us a good start. Jan and Peter watched the wake and called out directions, while I kept on some imaginary occult kind of a straight line. I was just trying to decide what effect the tide was having on us when Jan called out, "I see trees!" Trees were supposed to be ahead of us.

"I s-s-ssee a lighthouse!" stuttered Peter, trying to get it out before Jan did.

I kicked the boat out of gear, and stared at the light looming above us . . . same height, same cliff — there was no doubt about it, it was the same light.

So we had to give up trying to get across the strait, and stay on the side we had started from. Later in the day, we followed the curve of the shore into what I was afraid might be an unwanted channel. But it turned out to be a booming-ground, with at least four big booms tied up to the piles. It seemed a good idea to stay right there until we could find out where we were.

Booms are very handy, and quite all right to tie up to for the night. But you must be willing to accept their disadvantages as well.

Children love booms — but mustn't be allowed to play on them. The great sections of floating logs look compact and solid, but any one of the logs, if stepped on, might roll over and catch you in between. Or open out a gap and throw you into the water — then close over you again. A log up to five feet in diameter and fifty or eighty feet long is not a thing to fool with. Without a peavy and help of some kind you would be practically powerless to get a child out, if one had ever gone under the logs. Yet booms have an irresistible attraction for children.

Wasps love them too — these yellow-and-black-striped, lethal creatures are wonderful paper makers. They take mouthfuls of wood off the logs and chew it up with their formic acid (I suppose, I haven't looked it up in the "Encyclopædia Britannica," yet). But anyway, the result is the thin grey paper material that they build their big hanging nests with. The queen wasp starts it off — she being the only one that survives the winter. The start is just a tiny grey paper thing, not any bigger than a bantam egg. She carefully makes a certain number of cells in the prescribed manner inside, and lays an egg in each one. Then sits down and waits, having done the only stint of actual labour she has to do in her whole life.

Then from each cell comes forth a worker-wasp, a ready-made slave for the queen. She claps her hands, or her feet, and the workers run to groom and feed her. Then they start chewing more wood to make more cells for the queen to lay more eggs in. As the workers increase, the cells increase — round and round and round, and the wasps on the booms increase. They have to eat as well . . . and the simplest way is to come on board when they smell our food cooking and help themselves.

Tugs love booms — they love to collect them in the middle of the night. You are awakened up by a searchlight and a shrill "Toot-toot-toot." They are just as disgusted to see you as you are to see them. They have tied a tow-rope onto a string of sections, each 80 feet wide by perhaps 160 feet long, and may want to take ten of them together.

There is nothing you can do, except climb out on the slippery logs and try to get your ropes off. You have suspended your boat half-way between the ends of a section — the ends being the only place where there are coupling chains to tie on to. As long as you are beside the boat, you are all right — you can put one hand on the boat. But after that you just have to balance, and a boom-log in the dark seems as narrow as a tight-rope. You have safely made about fifteen feet of it, when the tugmen suddenly shine their searchlight on you — and you stand there teetering — completely blinded. After a few minutes they realize what they are doing — that it is not modesty that is making you wave your arms round in front of your face. The searchlight turns aside, and you make the last ten feet and grab the ring-bolt — then untie your rope.

Once you manage to get back to the boat with the wet slimy rope, then you can pull the boat up to where you are tied at the other end. You just manage to get that untied when the tug toots again, signifying that it is tired of waiting. You spring and clamber back onto the deck and grab a pike pole to fend off with. They turn the spotlight on you again, and you wave to let them know you are all clear. The whole boom moves slowly . . . out past you . . . and you are left forsaken and drifting in the dark. With a boat full of sleeping children it is easier to tow the boat than start up the engine. The seat of the dinghy is very wet, and your feet are clamped tight on a coil of wet rope. You tow the boat slowly towards the next boom — if there is one, or perhaps a pile that your boom was held by.

That night, however, we had no boom troubles. We rowed into the beach before dark. There were several big streams and the beach was covered with smooth round stones — loosely piled, just as they had come down with the spring freshets. We should have liked to explore a bit, but the fog was turning to rain; and we soon crowded back into the boat to get dry.

It was some time during the darkest part of that dark night that we were all suddenly jolted out of deep sleep by the most blood-curdling yowls from the beach — like a cat, but magnified fifty times.

"Mummy! Mummy! What is it?" called terrified voices.

"Listen . . . ." I shu-ushed. You could hear the knock, knock of the round stones as some soft foot trod on them.

Then again the long drawn-out yowl of a beast in sorrow . . . calling for something he couldn't find. Again we all shivered in terror, and again the stones tipped and knocked.

"I'm sure it wouldn't yowl like that if it were hunting," I said, but it didn't make us feel much happier.

From one end of the beach to the other it wandered — every now and then letting off a wail.

"Mummy! That one was closer!" called Jan from her bunk in the bow. It certainly was . . . . I grabbed the flashlight and swung its beam across the boom. Two yellow eyes . . . definitely nearer than the shore. Then they disappeared, and once more the stones rattled. After that I kept turning on the flash whenever the yowls seemed closer.

I had just swung the light along the shore when two shots rang out — there was a strangled sort of snarl — then the sound of men's voices. We sat for another half-hour, listening; and then went back to sleep.

Next morning we saw two men working on the booms near the shore and rowed round to talk to them. It was they who had shot the cougar in the night. They had shot its mate two nights before, when it had killed their dog right on the porch of their cabin, which was on the high point at one end of the bay.

"We were glad you kept turning on your flash," they said. "That gave us our chance to shoot."

Engines

E HAD JUST GOT THROUGH LEWIS CHANNEL, BETWEEN Redonda and the north end of Cortes Island, and had hardly worked round Bullock Point and got out of the tide which was bothering us — when the engine stopped. It was almost dark, nine-thirty, and we were still five miles from the inlet on the north side of Cortes, and there was no place else to go. I cranked and cranked, again and again — evidently there was something really wrong. I couldn't crank and watch the engine at the same time, so it was hard to find out just what it was. We couldn't stay where we were. There was just one continuous cliff and forty-seven fathoms right off it. There was nothing else to do but tow the boat the five miles to the inlet.

I helped John into his sleeping bag, in spite of his pleas that he was not sleepy; told Jan to steer and follow the dinghy — and took Peter with me in the dinghy. There was a slight current with us, which might increase later if the tide ebbed that way. It might go either way; for we were close to where the tides from the south met the tides from the north. The tides in these minor channels could easily vary in direction according to their height.

There was no use trying to hurry — we had a long pull ahead of us. If it were not blowing at this hour, it was not likely to later. If it did blow, it would be just too bad. I settled down to a short

103

steady stroke, trying not to let the rope slacken. If it did, you took the weight suddenly on your shoulders and neck. After two hours, I had a rest, ate some peanut butter, and made Peter go to bed. Then, with Jan, we looked at the chart again. We decided that we could probably anchor in a cove where the cliff ended, about a mile our side of the entrance to the inlet. That would leave only about one more mile. It had taken two hours to come less than three miles.

I told Jan to use the flash in half an hour's time to try to pick out the end of the cliff and the beginning of the cove. In about three-quarters of an hour she hailed me and shone the light again for me to see for myself. That was obviously the end of the cliff, and there was the cove beyond. I kept on for some distance, and then turned in at about the centre of the cove. The arms of the cove gradually folded about us and shut out the wide sea . . . . I let the boat gradually lose way, and sounded with a fish-line. Two . . . three . . . four fathoms. I let the anchor down slowly — worked my way along the side deck, and stepped on board. Jan was already in her bunk. She must be tired too — it was a long watch for a small girl, but I couldn't have managed alone. I crawled into my bag . . . could anyone as tired as I was possibly recover?

It was nine the next morning before we woke. I looked over the engine while I drank my second cup of coffee and soon found out what was wrong — a pin had come out of the coupling on the timing shaft that ran off the magneto. Another look at the breeze that was coming up, and I decided that I should have to tow another mile into the inlet. There we would be completely sheltered; there was a stream of fresh water, and I could take my time over the engine. The missing pin meant that the whole inner workings of the engine were upset. It might mean quite a long job.

In the end it was about a two-mile tow, because I wanted to get in as far as the stream. The tide was flooding into the inlet, so after I limbered up a little, it wasn't so bad. Once anchored, we got into our bathing suits, put all our clothes into a pool in the stream to soak, and tumbled into the lukewarm sea water.

After lunch, the children went ashore to tread out their clothes and get them out to dry. I went reluctantly into the engine room and had a tentative look at the engine. I wasn't in any particular hurry to find out that I didn't know how to re-time an engine. As long as I thought I could, I was reasonably cheerful. After all, I knew the theory of the thing. It would have been sheer madness to take the trips on the part of the coast where we did unless I knew something about an engine. After a lot of thinking I decided to leave it until the next day. I was stiff and tired with the towing, and I hadn't got to bed until after two that morning.

We swam and fished, and caught a good-sized salmon. We lay in the sun. We explored. Jan and Peter rowed back, all excited, saying that they had found a salt water waterfall. So John and I had to row back with them to see it too. There was about a six foot fall, and it was perfectly salt. It must fill at high tide. We climbed up beside the fall, but it was impossible to explore. It just disappeared round corners, like a meandering lake, but salt. I think it must have had another, wider entrance somewhere. Cortes is a very large island, with many deep bays and gorges. On the chart, this salt water lake is just marked with a circle of unexplored dots. The dots would have to remain — we couldn't explore it either.

That evening we made a fire on the sloping rocks and ate our supper on shore. We grilled salmon steaks over the hot bark embers, and ate without benefit of forks or knives. It is really the only way I enjoy fish, fresh from the sea, to the grid, and eaten round a fire on the beach.

The sparks floated up like fireflies in the quiet darkness. Then I had to tell the children what fireflies were and describe them. We don't have them on the Pacific coast. A grouse was drumming on some tree or log. We had a guessing game on what direction it was coming from. One moment you could swear it was coming out of the rocks you were sitting on. Then it would be somewhere from overhead . . . then back in the woods again. It was quite unearthly, and vaguely disturbing. When the granite under our fire exploded with a loud bang, John said he thought he would like to go to bed. The other two didn't argue at all . . . we rowed out to the boat, and the grouse drummed no more.

I lay in my bag, long after the children were asleep, thinking about the engine. I hoped my subconscious mind would sort it all out, in the night, better than I could.

I put the children ashore after breakfast with strict orders that I was to be left alone and not interrupted.

"We wouldn't even want to," said Peter, sitting down on a point as close to the boat as he could get — he likes to hand me wrenches.

Engines were invented and reared by men. They are used to being sworn at, and just take advantage of you; if you are polite to them — you get absolutely nowhere. The children were better on shore. Peter would soon get tired of sitting there.

I sat on my heels, cursing softly when the wrench slipped and took a chunk off my knuckle. Finally the sparkplug co-operated, and came out with the porcelain still intact. Then I stuck the screwdriver through the hole and felt around for No. 1 piston. That piston seemed quite inert . . . but after some turns of the flywheel it came up on top. No. 1 valve should be either opening or closing, I wasn't sure which. The only valve I could see through the small hole was doing either one or the other. Then I decided that that part of the internal workings must be coupled together and had probably not been upset . . . well and good.

Then I turned to the shaft where the pin had come out of the coupling. "Hell's bells!" All that bother with No. 1 piston being on top dead centre would be wasted if it didn't fire at that moment . . . the magneto must be the key to the whole thing. The engine was an old four-cylinder Kermath with a low-tension magneto. The distributor was on the face of the magneto, and the wires from the sparkplugs led down to the distributor . . . . (Dots for a very long time.) Then I found that, by turning the shaft by hand until opening of the points on the magneto coincided with No. 1 lead, then No. 1 sparkplug at the end of that wire — fired.

I made myself a cup of coffee and drank it while thinking that one over — I wasn't quite ready to believe it yet. It seemed just a little too easy to be true. Then I remembered my subconscious that had worked all night on the subject, and I rather grudgingly gave it the credit, while all the glory I had was a bashed knuckle. I finally committed my subconscious and me, put a nail in place of the errant pin in the coupling, and secured it with some electric tape. Good! That hadn't been so hard. Everyone should know how before they go off cruising in a boat. On the other hand, this had taken years to happen: I might have been worrying all that time if I had known it could happen.

I connected the battery, I turned on the switch, I consulted my subconscious, and I pulled the crank . . . . The most awful backfire shook the boat from stem to stern. Looking towards the shore, I could see the children jumping up and down and could see that they were shouting, but I couldn't hear them . . . . I switched off and sat down limply — I was completely shattered.

I called to my agitated children to come out and have a cup of tea. I would have to think it out before I took a chance with another bang like that . . . . The children looked a little dubious about coming on board at all. John asked to see the blood — a bang is not a bang to him unless there is blood. I showed him my knuckle, which quite satisfied him.

Then I sorted out the jumble of things I knew about engines . . . and of course it must have fired on the exhaust stroke. If I turned the engine over until No. 1 came on top again, perhaps that would be the firing stroke. No, that would still be firing on exhaust stroke. Out came the nail again and I redid all that part. Only then did I remember that the markings on my flywheel would have told me quite a bit. The subconscious is all very well, but it is sometimes not very practical.

The children fled to the safety of the shore. I put in my rubber earplugs — switched on — and pulled her up. At first I wasn't sure if anything had happened — but there was the flywheel whizzing round. Then I remembered the earplugs . . . there she was . . . purring away. Me and my subconscious solemnly shook hands.

The engine is normally so well checked over in the spring that nothing very much is likely to happen — I am sure the pin will never come out of that shaft again. But there is no accounting for dry batteries. The engine started on coil ignition from a dry battery, and then I, personally, had to switch it over to magneto. That was one of Peter's chief duties as mate — to see that I had made the switch. He used to get rather bored, as I hardly ever forgot. So now and again I would pretend to and he would feel most important.

Then the life of dry batteries seems to vary — or I like to think it does and so divide the blame.

We had spent two weeks poking into all the unknown bays and inlets to the north of the approach to Knight Inlet, checking on all the white-shell beaches, and generally exploring.

Then our bread gave out, and the sourdough that old Mike had given me died (I forgot to feed it) and we had to find some place for provisions. If we left in time, before the fishermen got all the fresh provisions, we should be able to get bread. There were only two trading stores and gas in half a day's run — one away over off Blackfish Sound, and the other back on Minstrel Island.

So, we packed up the boat for running. Peter was shortening up the dinghy rope, Jan had pulled out the chart, and John had climbed up on the steering seat.

"All set?" I asked, glancing round.

I pulled the rear starter up sharply. Again — and again — and again. "If it isn't spark, it's gas, and if it isn't gas it's spark." I reminded myself. I checked the gas tank, and the shut-off valve. I raised the float-level in the carburetor and enriched the mixture a little. I switched on and tried again . . . so it must be spark. I took a terminal off the battery and tried the spark . . . the most sickly, yellow, slow spark.

"You may as well go on shore and play," I said. "The battery is practically dead."

They looked at each other silently — and faded away.

We were at least thirty miles from where there was any hope of finding another dry battery. There was practically no chance of another boat passing our way — to get a tow. We had purposely gone where we would be by ourselves.

I put the battery out on deck in the sun. I polished the terminals. I took out all the sparkplugs and cleaned them. Knocked their points a little closer, and laid them all out in the sun with the battery to get hot. I would give everything another hour to really heat up — including the engine room, before I tried again.

I studied the chart — it would have been impossible to find a more out of the way place, or a more awkward place to try to tow a boat. By cheating a little in measuring the course I gained three miles. But in terms of trying to tow a twenty-five foot boat — it didn't help much. If I got the engine started, and made for Blackfish Sound, we would likely strike wind. We couldn't stop and take shelter, for I might never get started again. If we headed for Minstrel we would strike bad tides — but it was the only possible place to tow to; so either way, it had better be Minstrel.

I reached for the tide book. Tides would have to be worked out chiefly in relation to towing. I couldn't possibly tow more than one tide — so there had to be a good place to hole up for the night at the end of six hours . . . that meant waiting here until noon. That would be better, even if the engine started.

I called for someone to come out and get me. Then I lay on the beach and tried to think how many hours' rowing it would take to tow the boat thirty miles — even with the tide. By the time the tide was at the right stage to try the engine again, I had used up enough energy thinking about it to have towed the boat there and back.

We rowed off to the boat. I rechecked everything. I connected the hot battery — I primed each cylinder with naphtha gas — I screwed in each hot sparkplug. Then I pulled up hard on the crank. "Grr-r-r-r-p-p-p," she started, and when I hurriedly threw the switch over onto magneto she settled down with a melodious "pur-r-r."

I nursed that throttle for ten minutes before I dared to leave it long enough to pull up the anchor. If she faltered, I should never be able to get to the throttle from the forward deck in time.

We were all singing as we worked our way out of that god-forsaken little hole. For the moment, I had lost my taste for places where no one else ever went — a state of mind begotten of a dead battery.

Old Phil

HIL LAVINE, THE OLD FRENCHMAN IN LAURA COVE, WAS full of calamities when we ran in to see him in July. He had had a bad winter. In the late fall he had something wrong with him, and had to go into the hospital at Powell River for a while. Then he had to come home sooner than he should have because the fisherman who was looking after his place for him wouldn't stay any longer on account of the cougars.

Then Mike's old place in Melanie Cove had been taken over by some fellow from Vancouver.

"A city man," said Phil scornfully, "'e didn' know 'ow to live

109

in country like dis — 'e was scared to deat' all de time."

In April, fish-boats that tried to anchor close in in Melanie Cove — the way they did in old Mike's time — complained that someone was taking potshots at them. No one was hurt, and the police were a little sceptical.

"I knowed it was de trut'," Phil said. "Dat fellow was gettin' more crazy every day."

The climax came one day when the fellow suddenly appeared and pushed his way into Phil's cabin, with his rifle in his arms. Old Phil was sitting in front of the stove, smoking. The man didn't say anything, but sat down in a chair opposite Phil with his gun across his knees, his finger on the trigger.

"'is eyes were crazy," said Phil. "I t'ought it was de end of me." Every time he tried to talk to the man, he pointed the gun at him. They sat there all afternoon — Phil smoking, but otherwise afraid to move.

Finally, the man, who had been getting more and more agitated, said, "Phil, you won't laugh at me, will you?"

"My God!" Phil stuttered, "I ain't got nuttin' to laugh about!" and then added quietly, "I'll make up de fire, an' you stay an' 'ave supper wid me."

The man let him get up, and he made up the fire and put the kettle on. He continued talking quietly to him, and the man gradually relaxed.

Phil finally decided to risk it . . . he put the pot of stew on the stove, brought an armful of wood in from outside the door; he filled a tin with grain from a sack under the table, said he had to feed the hens before it got dark, and asked the man to watch the fire and stir the stew.

Then, still talking, he opened the door and went out and over to the hen house. He didn't dare look back to see if he were being watched, but once round the end of the hen house where he couldn't be seen from the house, he put the tin down and took the trail to the woods at a run. "I knowed I 'ad to get out of gun range before 'e discovered I weren't comin' back."

He had a small mountain to climb before he could get help from anyone. It was only a rambling goat-trail, and it was dark when he finally stumbled into the Salter place. The two old brothers finally interpreted Phil's French, gasps and signs — he had no

English left. The three of them fell into the old fish-boat and didn't stop until they reached Bliss Landing four hours later, and got in touch with the police boat.

"An' we stayed right der until de police take 'im away. 'e was quite crazy, and now 'e's locked up for good," said Phil, rubbing his hands.

Phil was out of tobacco, and he was drying some green tobacco leaves over the stove — trying to hurry them up. Long before tobacco was produced commercially in Canada, the French habitants or farmers in the country districts of Quebec all had their own little tobacco patch, and grew and cured their tobacco for the winter. Phil had brought this frugal habit with him from Quebec. He showed us the little drying shed he had outside, where bunches of tobacco leaves hung from poles, drying slowly.

A baby goat bunted me suddenly and expertly, and the children laughed. I bunted him back with my fists and he jumped straight up in the air and landed with his four little black hooves bunched together.

"No more cougars, Phil?" I asked.

He pointed to two skins to the end of the woodshed, and shrugged: "Always de cougar, but wort' forty-dollar bounty."

Coastwise

OMEONE AT BLISS LANDING, HEARING THAT WE WERE going up Toba Inlet, asked if we would leave a message for two brothers who had a small place on Homfray Channel, which was on our way to Toba. We spent a couple of days in Melanie Cove where old Mike lives, and then set out along the shore of Homfray to try to find the place. The shores were very steep and rocky, and disappeared down into the sea at the same angle — one of these no-bottom shores. Then in a bit of a bay we saw a small float, tight up against the shore, held off with poles. A fish-boat was tied alongside.

We had just tied up when one of the brothers came down to the float. I gave him the message, and as he was very insistent, we followed him up to the hidden cabin.

We were quite unprepared for what we found. I had thought they were probably fishermen, with a small summer shack. But evidently they lived here all the year round and only fished occasionally. The cabin was quite large, and neat. Half a dozen loaves of bread, just out of the oven, were cooling on the table, and jars there were of fresh cherry jam. This brother did all the cooking and kept house. We sat down for tea with him — hot bread, honey from their own hives, butter from their goats.

Before we were finished, the other brother came bounding in — a regular dynamo of a man. I have never seen so much seething energy in anyone. And full of what his brother called his "schemes."

They showed us all over the place. There were acres of walnut trees, just beginning to bear and now too big to transplant. One of his schemes — he had expected to sell the trees and make thousands of dollars out of them. Something had gone wrong — too expensive to get them to the right market or something.

Then there was trench after trench of Cascara saplings, now five or six feet high and hopelessly crowded. He had intended to set out a plantation of them, but the price of Cascara bark had dropped so low that it wasn't worth bothering with. If he had set them out, the price later was so high that he would have made his thousands out of them. He seemed to be a man that conceived and rose to tremendous crests, but was not capable of being interested in the troughs that surely followed.

They had a wonderful vegetable garden. Water was piped down from the mountains in three-inch pipes, and the growth was prodigious. Then we had to climb up to the spring from which they piped water to the cabin. There was a small pool at the source, perhaps about four feet by four, made by a low dam. And in the small pool lived a fourteen-inch trout. It had been put in the pool as a fingerling and had lived there for almost five years.

It rose to the surface as soon as we leant over the pool. The quiet brother took a crust out of his pocket and scattered crumbs on the surface. The trout made great swirls and ate them eagerly. It looked sleek and healthy but must have missed all the best of a fish's life. If it were turned loose now in a stream it would have no instincts of any kind. Any fisherman could catch it in a landing net without bothering with a lure.

We returned to the cabin by another path, under trees laden with cherries. The children were turned loose with a pail to fill with cherries to take back with us, as well as all they could eat.

Weekly the brothers took a load of fruit and vegetables to logging camps ten to twenty-five miles away. The quiet brother canned and bottled all they could eat for the winter. The rest they gave away or it was wasted. "There's enough of everything for an army," the quiet brother groaned. But there was always another plan ahead for the dynamic dreamer — something that kept him glowing with vigour.

The quiet brother showed me their storehouse — double walled, of logs. In the dark cool interior were shelves full of bottled venison and salmon — pickled beets and onions — bottles of fruit. Lastly, a roothouse all ready for the fall root crop.

All that was the quiet brother's achievement — survival in the wilderness with practically no money. I know of two couples who tried this living off the country and what you can produce — as an experiment to see if it could be done. One was a writer, and he and his wife and two children tried it for a year. They proved that it could be done, if you had or could make about thirty-five dollars a month for clothes, sugar, flour — things you couldn't produce. However, they owned their own place and already had a garden. They knew how to fish and hunt and can the surplus. And the beach in front of their place was covered with driftwood. I think they had had the idea of starting a back-to-the-woods campaign for people living in town on relief. Most city dwellers could not have done it at all.

We bought all the vegetables the boat would hold from the brothers, but had to accept the pail of cherries and a loaf of home-made bread. And also to give a promise that we would call in again.

At the very last moment, when we were talking on the wharf, they spoiled our trip up Toba. As soon as I mentioned that we were heading up Toba, they were all against it. Did I know that there was no anchorage of any kind, except in Salmon River? And Salmon River at this time of the year was full of cinnamon bears after the salmon. They were light brown in colour, and more like the grizzlies in habits. Also, they were very aggressive, and apt to charge you on sight. We shouldn't be able to get off the boat.

Well, I only half believed it all, but they had fished up there a good many years, and should know. I had also been told by others that the head of the inlet was low and swampy and bad for mosquitoes, and so we gave up the idea.

Instead, we went on up to the Yucultas and tied up at the wharf of people we knew in the big bay half-way up Stuart Island. You get quite a swirl and strong current when the rapids are running at their hardest, but it is perfectly safe. There were two little girls there who were being brought up by their grandmother. We used to walk back with them to a lake in the interior of the island to swim. It was a peculiar little lake in the middle of what I think must be muskeg. The muskeg was all right if you kept walking. But if you didn't you began to sink. So we would change into our bathing suits while on the move, hang our clothes on a bush, and ooze into the water, which was warm and very soft. I don't think the lake was very deep, we never investigated closely. We didn't like that bottom — it was soft and sinking, and full of unknowns.

I left all the children playing together one evening, and went off with the father and an older boy to watch them fish with lines at the edge of the whirlpools. We used an open gas-boat they had, and shot round the S.E. point that swings out to the edge of the rapids. Then they worked out of the current and up the back currents into the little bay just beyond the point. There they had an old scow tied up. It was anchored at one end by a line that went out into the swirls of the current as it swept round the point. The other end was tied to a tree on the shore.

We climbed on board, and they slacked off on the shore line and pulled the scow out on the anchored line until they were just on the edge of where the whirlpools formed. They baited the fishing line by cutting a herring in half and running a wire lead through the tail half, and then attaching a hook — no weights, no spoons. The current was so strong that it carried the line out and down, and the current kept the herring tail wagging and spinning. The pull was so hard that I was sure I had a ten-pounder on from the very start. The scow twisted this way and that way, and when they saw an extra large whirlpool approaching, the men would slack off on the anchor end and rapidly pull us out of reach with the shore line. You could see right down the whirlpool's throat as it sucked and reached at us. Then off it would twirl, and we would pull ourselves out to the edge again.

There was a man fishing off the tip of the point just beyond us. He was on a high platform that stretched ten feet out over the water. Suddenly, with a great shout, he started pulling in his line. You don't play your fish with this kind of fishing — you use a wire lead and a heavy line, and haul. That man fought his line for fifteen minutes before he finally got his fish clear of the water and up onto the narrow platform. Then, before he could gaff it, the hook evidently worked out, for with a yell the man flung himself on the fish, and sat there with it clasped in his arms, laughing and shouting for help. Someone came out to his rescue and they got the big spring salmon to shore.

"At least a sixty-pounder," the man with me said.

A minute later he was himself busy trying to land a thirty-pounder. The boy shouted, and I grabbed the shore line and helped him pull the scow out of danger. I think the man would have let us sink rather than lose his fish.

Then it was too dark to fish any longer and the water was running too hard — and we walked home through the woods.

Johnstone Straits were running white — and it wasn't any fun. So we turned off into a narrow harbour to wait it out. We waited for a couple of days, tied up to a long float that keeled over when the wind hit, and was difficult to walk on.

It was three in the morning when something woke me ... someone calling me .... I hastily opened the canvas curtain and looked out. The girl from the house on the hill was kneeling on the wharf in the grey light — her hair blowing out behind her. Her mother, who was rather frail, had been ill all night, with a severe and continuous nose bleed. The *Columbia*, the Coast Mission boat, with a doctor on board, would be passing early in the morning. If she could be intercepted they could get help. We were the only boat in the harbour; did I think I could get down to Salmon River where they had a radio-telephone? We looked at the tide book with the flashlight, and I said we would try it when the tide turned at about four o'clock. Salmon River was some ten miles down the straits, and the water from the river makes a tide-rip as it hits the heavy tides of Johnstone Strait — it would be easier to get into the basin if I could reach there near slack water.

I woke up the children and we ate our breakfast and then pushed off. The tide had not yet turned, but the wind was behind us and there was not much sea yet. I ran full-out, and it took us only about an hour to get there. The entrance is narrow but there is a fair-sized basin when you get through. There was an adequate wharf about twenty-five feet above my head, sitting on the edge of a mud bank — no water. I anchored the boat and took the dinghy. There was a slippery ramp over the mud bank up which I finally slithered.

It was the trading store that had the radio-telephone, and the storekeeper lived above — the girl had told me. I pounded and shouted for ten minutes before a man's furious face appeared at an upstairs window. He calmed down when I explained the emergency, and said he would contact the *Columbia* later — not much use trying before seven . . . . I pointed out that at seven I might not have been able to get there at all.

The girl wrote later to thank me — the *Columbia* had come in about nine. The doctor had managed to stop the haemorrhage and they had taken her off to the mission hospital.

The fish-boats used to do a lot of emergency handling of telegrams and messages. We once had one handed to us by a fisherman at the Yuculta Rapids. The telegram had been telephoned from Victoria to Campbell River up the island. From there it had been telephoned to Squirrel Cove on Cortes Island. Then it was handed over to a fish-boat to take up to Bruce's Landing on Stuart Island, and for them please to try to locate me.

At Bruce's Landing they told the fisherman that we had been in two days ago for gas, and that we might still be tied up at Asman's Bay. So, just by chance it reached us.

The telegram read — "Motor Launch Caprice, Bruce's Landing, via Squirrel Cove. Doctor M. advises Plactdndectomy Attendctony. Wire consent, Love B."

What was I to consent to? Whatever Dr. M. advised sounded more like a prehistoric animal of the pre-glacial period than a disease. Everyone looked at the telegram and had a guess. A fisherman said, "I think I know what that is. It's a boy, isn't it?"

"It's a girl," I said, and I never heard what he suspected.

But I had to get to a telephone even to wire, and the nearest one was back in Squirrel Cove. It took us a full day to get there as the tides at the Yucultas were wrong. I telephoned the doctor, for I simply had to know what awful thing I was consenting to.

The message, relayed by two country telephone operators, had grown in length by gathering strange letters in its course — he merely wanted to take her appendix out. I got a stay of execution by promising to be home in three days.

So, while there were disadvantages to the Coast Emergency Service, how thankful everybody was at times that they could count on it!

Of Things Unproved

E SCOURED THE SHALLOWS FOR A MONTH THAT SUMMER trying to find a seahorse. It seems a most unlikely thing to find in this latitude; but I read somewhere that one species had been found as far north as the English Channel. If in the English Channel, why not here?

Last year, after we got home, when we were looking up something else in the "Encyclopædia Britannica," Peter pounced on the picture of a seahorse and announced, "I saw one of those last year!"

I looked incredulous . . . . "I did, really, Jan saw it too." I turned my gaze on Jan . . . . Yes, Jan had seen it — but no one could remember where, beyond that it had been in a reedy, sandy place in shallow water. When I asked why on earth they hadn't called me to look at it, Peter furnished the last proof.

"Oh, it was just swinging there on a weed, holding on with its tail, and we were collecting sand dollars."

Jan said, "We did look for it again, but we couldn't find it. Peter said it was a greeny-brown just like the weeds."

When I asked if the head really looked like a horse, Jan said, "Well, it made you think of a horse." And Peter said, "Oh, it did too, Jan, it looked just like the one in the chess set." So the evidence was all there — everything but the place.

I set them to work trying to think. The sand dollars were the best clue, for we didn't often see any. The north end of Denman Island was the only place they could think of where they had

117

definitely found sand dollars — and also, we had been there that summer.

To go back through one whole summer, to the beginning of the summer before that, in a child's life, is just about a hopeless task. Sometimes I have chased down the years on a sure clue, looking for a source — only to find that it was something I had read to them; they had played around with it in their minds, thoroughly mixed it up with fantasy, and a couple of years later presented it to me as an actual fact. Which, I suddenly realize, is a fairly good description of a seahorse.

Another fantastic thing about seahorses is the way they have solved the problem of excess population in the seahorse world. Mother produces the eggs, but deposits them in a pouch on father's abdomen. It is father who goes around looking incredibly pregnant, for whatever length of time a seahorse's pregnancy lasts. They both look carefully after their young — most unfish-like.

So it ended in our spending a month in the following summer back-tracking up the Vancouver Island side of the Gulf, scouring the sandy bottoms and reedy bays — looking for seahorses swinging on green weeds.

Whenever I can, I do two things with one effort. If I have to move rocks or earth when building something, or gardening, or some like project — it makes me very unhappy just to cart them off anywhere to get rid of them. If I can take the rocks out from where they are not wanted and, with practically the same amount of energy that it takes to throw them away, build them into a rock wall or incorporate them in cement work — I am supremely happy.

So, in the month we spent looking for seahorses, I carried on a second project at the same time. While the children paddled for hours in the shallows among the weeds, very concerned with an unlikely fish for which I had offered a good reward, I concerned myself largely with — where had Juan de Fuca actually gone when he was on this coast in the 1590's?

Juan de Fuca's story of his trip has reached us in a very roundabout way. It comes to us first via a seafaring man named Michael Lok, who wrote of it or told it to Richard Hakluyt. Richard Hakluyt, "by reason of his great knowledge of geographic matters," and his acquaintance with "the chieftest captains at sea, the greatest merchants, and the best mariners of our [English] nation," was selected to go to Paris in 1583 with the English Ambassador, as Chaplain. It was there, on instructions, that he occupied himself chiefly in collecting information of the Spanish and French movements, and "making diligent inquiries of such things as might yield light unto our western discovery of America."

Hakluyt, who was at Christ Church, Oxford, lectured in that university on geography and "shewed the old imperfectly composed, and the new lately reformed mappes, globes, spheres, and other instruments of this art." He wrote two or three books, as well as making translations from the Portuguese.

When he died, in 1616, a number of Hakluyt's manuscripts, enough to form a fourth volume, fell into the hands of the Rev. Samuel Purchas — another divine interested in geography and discoveries. These manuscripts he published, in abridged form, in 1622 under the title *Hakluytus Posthumus, or Purchas his Pilgrimes.*

Until his death Hakluyt was incessantly employed in the collection, examination and translation of accounts of voyages and travels, and in correspondence with men anxious to receive and impart information — among them Sir Philip Sidney, Sir Francis Walsingham and Sir Francis Drake; also the cartographers Ortelius and Mercator.

So Juan de Fuca's account of his voyage up the coast of British Columbia came down to us through someone who was used to examining and weighing reports that were either told to or sent to him.

In 1592, Michael Lok met Juan de Fuca in the Mediterranean. Juan de Fuca was a Greek by birth, but he told Lok that he had acted as pilot for the Spaniards in the Caribbean for forty years — so we can assume that Spanish was his language. He told Lok that he had been "sent out in 1592, by the Viceroy of Mexico, with a small caravel and Pinace, armed with mariners only, to find the supposed Straits of Anian, and the passage thereof into the Sea they call the North Sea — which is our North West Sea."

He showed Lok the course he took — along the coast of New Spain (Mexico) and California, and the Indies now called North

America. Lok says, "All of which voyage he signified to me in a great map or sea-card of mine own, which I had laid before him."

Juan de Fuca continued up the coast until, Lok reports, "He came to a broad Inlet of the sea between 47 and 48 Lat. He entered there into, sayling therein for more than twenty days and found that land trending still sometimes N.W. and N.E. and N. and also E. and S.E. and a very much broader Sea than at the said entrance — and that he went by divers islands in that sayling."

If they had rowed and sailed along the north shore of that broad inlet and by divers islands for twenty days — where would they likely have got to? Vancouver with the *Discovery* and the *Chatham*, big ships compared to the caravel, had followed the south shore right into Puget Sound, landlocked by all the Puget Sound islands; and had continued north on the mainland side frantically trying to find a passage through the mountains.

Juan de Fuca in his smaller ships would likely have followed the tides on the north shore and turned N.W. up by San Juan, "and other divers islands." Somewhere close to Nanaimo, he would have emerged "into a much broader sea than at the said entrance [Flattery]" and all the Gulf of Georgia would suddenly have lain before him.

If he had sailed north, and north-west up the Vancouver Island side of the Gulf, in twenty days of rowing and sailing, from where he entered the broad inlet of the sea, he would have been about at Texada Island. Texada Island, at the south end, is where the Gulf of Georgia ends and narrows down into Stevens Pass, or a still narrower pass inside Denman Island.

Now, Juan de Fuca says, "At the entrance to said Strait, there is on the north-west coast thereof, a great headland or island, with an exceeding high pinnacle or spired rock thereon."

There are really two islands there, although from the shore of Vancouver Island they appear as one. Lasqueti Island, about nine miles long and two wide, is close to the southern end of Texada Island, which is twenty-seven miles long and four wide.

The *Coast Pilot*, speaking of Texada, says, "The south-east extremity of Texada is rugged and precipitous . . . almost immediately over it rises Mount Dick, a very remarkable hump-shaped hill 1,130 feet high." About Lasqueti, it says, "Mount Trematon, a singular turret-shaped summit, 1,050 feet high rises nearly at its centre."

That is what we were looking at as we approached, and it is what Juan de Fuca and his men would have seen on the north-west side of the gulf at the entrance to the straits.

Twenty miles from the north end of Texada he would have entered the south end of Johnstone Strait. Averaging one to one and a half miles in width, they ran for one hundred miles. Beyond mentioning that they had landed on the shore and found "Natives clad in skins of beasts," Juan next says, "that being entered thus far into the said Straits and being come to the North Sea already, and finding the sea wide enough everywhere, and to be thirty or forty leagues wide — he thought he had well discharged his office and done the thing he had been sent to do." In other words he thought he had found the supposed Straits of Anian, and the passage thereof into the North Sea.

Out at Cape Flattery, the entrance to what Captain Vancouver called the Strait of Juan de Fuca, there is no such island or headland, nor turret-shaped rock. And Juan de Fuca referred to it as a broad inlet of the sea — not a strait.

Vancouver says: "The entrance which I have called the supposed Straits of Juan de Fuca, instead of being between 47 and 48, is between 48 and 49, and leads not into a far broader sea or Mediterranean Ocean." Later, since he couldn't find the turret or pinnacle, he came to the conclusion that Juan had never been there at all.

Still no seahorses, and the youngsters' legs were getting a waterlogged look from so much wading. But it was not lost time, for they found and learned about many other things.

John came along the beach to me, grumbling, "Everything I find, they say it isn't — and I think it is."

"Well, never mind," I consoled. "I don't suppose anyone will believe that what I have found — is what I think it is."

"Well, then," said John happily, "I can say that I found a seahorse — and you can say that you found . . . what were you looking for anyway, Mummy?"

"I don't really know."

Mistaken Island

T WAS A FISHERMAN WHO LED US THROUGH THE REEFS and hidden dangers into the little anchorage in the middle of the Winchelsea Islets. We had been hanging round the edge of the Gulf of Georgia since seven in the morning, hoping to make the twenty-five miles crossing to the mainland. There is no use getting impatient with a gulf — it just rolls on and on, and takes its own time about calming down. June is an uncertain month for weather on the coast of British Columbia. It has not yet established any definite pattern. The glass had just been sulky for the last couple of days — doing neither one thing nor the other, and giving no clues. There had been a medium south-easter, which might have petered out at any time. Instead, it was blowing harder than ever.

In July, when the glass had steadied to 31 and the light westerlies are established, guessing changes to almost certainty. If the glass drops suddenly to 29 or below, with a clear sky and a glassy roll starting from the south-east, you know that you have about two and a half hours to get across the gulf before it starts blowing. You go, if you are in a hurry. Otherwise, you do something else for three days until it blows itself out.

This early June we had got tired of guessing, so had gone out to have a closer look. But there it was — rolling white and sullen, and obviously going to be worse. So we turned back and headed up towards Nanoose. We must have looked a little lost or forlorn; for when the fishing boat overtook us, the man called out that if we wanted a good place to hole up in we should follow him.

He led us by a deep, narrow channel, through a maze of reefs and foul ground, into a little circular haven protected by two small islands and three little islets.

"Good place to know," he said, when we had our anchors down. "Safe in any blow." I noticed that he dropped a stern anchor as well. There certainly wasn't very much room to swing, but there was perfect shelter.

We fastened down some curtains and made hot cocoa and toast to warm ourselves up. The bells on the fish-boat was tinkling and tinkling . . . and John said it was like reindeer.

I don't think they fish commercially in other seas the way they fish on this coast. The boat anchored beside us was a troller — about thirty-two feet in length, with a canoe stern, a mast amidships, and directly in front of the mast, a small wheelhouse. When you enter the wheelhouse, steps lead directly down below into the cabin. The part of the wheelhouse not taken up with steps houses the steering seat and wheel. The engine is underneath the wheelhouse and the steps. The cabin has a couple of bunks, a dropleaf table and a stove — and all the owner's belongings. The cabin roof is raised, to give headroom, to within four feet of the bow.

The after-half of the boat is taken up with holds for the ice and fish. Hatch-covers make it like a flush deck. Two long rigid fishing poles are fastened to, and extend some distance above the mast. These are let down by tackles, and extend at right angles out from the boat — one on each side. Each pole has three fishing lines at, say, four-foot intervals, running through pulleys and back to the boat. By varying the amount of lead on each line they are kept at selected depths.

They use different lures — flashers, wobblers, plugs, with or without bait. Each pulley on the pole has a small round bell attached to it, which jingles wildly when a fish strikes that line. Then the fisherman raises the pole until he can grab the right line and pull it in by hand. Fishermen who can afford it now have an arrangement of cogs, spindles and levers that run off the engine. By throwing the right lever, the line they want winds in — making everything easier if there is only one man aboard. You see the fishing boats coming in, followed by the seagulls screaming and wheeling, landing in the water to fight for bits — the men are gutting the fish on the way to the anchorage or the packer, and putting them in ice down in the hold.

There is a lot of superstition among the fishermen — lucky boats, unlucky boats. They all watch the lucky boat — trail along behind, trying to share a little of whatever it is she has .... They will tell you that a certain woman, on a certain boat, has lucky hands — electricity, magnetism, or something. She can tend the lines on one side of the boat, her husband on the other — but she catches all the fish. Then the propellers. Some propellers have a certain ring about them that attracts the fish. The note of others repels them. After a run of bad luck a man will replace his propeller, if he can, and his luck will change. All this is probably more rife among the boats that are out for a whole season. They are out of touch with everything and everybody except other fishermen in other boats. They hole up at night in some sheltered bay, visit each other's boats, drink coffee and swap yarns . . . . The superstitions grow and spread.

Our fisherman had eaten, and had now turned in to sleep — he had been out since three in the morning, fishing around the reefs off Gabriola. A hard life — but now he slept, and his bells were quiet.

I landed the children and they ran over to the other side of the island to play where they wouldn't disturb the fisherman. They were back in about an hour's time, all grinning and beckoning me to come ashore and see something. I sculled in. They had caught quite a big plaice or flounder, over a foot long. It had been cut off by the tide in a sandy pool, and my Red Indians had closed in for the kill.

"I saw its eyes peeking out of the sand," said John.

"It almost dumped me, when I stepped on it," said Peter.

"We took a long board," Jan said, "and crowded it into the edge."

Now they wanted to make a fire over on the beach and broil it. I gave them some matches, and they bounded off; then paused for a second to say that, if I came back in half an hour, I could have some too.

I can remember catching flounders on the wide tidal sand flats of the lower St. Lawrence when I was a child. We used to go out on the flats at low water, armed with sticks with needles embedded in the end — to spear the flounders as they came in with the tide. They were only about three inches long and the exact colour of the sand. Unless you saw the little muddy cloud they sent up when they moved, you could never spot them. "There she spouts!" we would yell, and stab at them, only to miss. Someone must once have stabbed one or we would never have been so persistent.

The best way to catch them was to trap them under your bare feet. The white feet must have attracted them. You would feel a mysterious little tickle under the arch. If you stooped quickly and put a hand on each side of your arch — then you would pull out a little browny-grey flounder. The harpoon men would call out, "Not fair," but one by one they would all change to "feet."

I don't know whether fish of the kind my youngsters caught grow up into halibut, or are young plaice. I believe that all these flat fish start out as ordinary, upright minnows. But suddenly the little halibut minnow starts to sag and twist. Everything in his body sags and twists, and he begins to lie more and more flat on the sand. I am glad that fish-mothers are completely lacking in the maternal instincts; for now, one of the baby's eyes — the right one — leaves it proper place and gradually climbs up on top and stays beside the other eye — giving it a slightly cross-eyed appearance. And worst of all, his mouth twists and draws up at one corner into a lopsided, sardonic smile. Of course there is no accounting for mothers — his might have preferred him that way.

I carried a billy of tea ashore, and bread, and we ate the flounder for lunch. Afterwards we wandered over the islands, picking different specimens of wild flowers to press in magazines. We found a row of little driftwood huts just above high-water mark, probably built by the hand trollers. When the fish are running in July and August, the hand trollers go off in rowboats and camp on the shore. They fish with two or three lines. Like the big trollers, they use their own pet lures — brass or nickel spinners or wobblers; sometimes wooden "plugs" that resemble some unknown shrimp-like monster, draped all over with hooks. We wondered what they did for fresh water on these little islands. Our fisherman told us later that when the fish are running, the fish-packer from the cannery comes every evening to collect the fish; and always carries water and provisions. Hand trollers of course had no ice, so their fish had to be collected sometimes twice a day.

Our fisherman woke up — but he didn't go out. It was too rough to troll. He sat with us, by our fire on the beach, for a while. He expected it to blow all night and drop in the morning.

"But it will still be rolling too high for you to get across tomorrow. It will probably slam around hard from the west when this stops, and that will kick up a filthy sea. Just be patient."

He had gone when we woke up in the morning. I had heard his engine start up in the very early hours; and then the jingle of the little bells .... Then the waves of his going had rocked me back to sleep.

The south-east wind had dropped, as he had predicted, and high clouds were moving from the west. Perhaps, by the afternoon, it would have made up its mind what it was going to do. In the meantime, I decided to run up to North-West Bay, roughly ten miles farther north. It is a peculiar coast just there: a deep channel right along the rocky shore; then, out beyond that, a foul stretch full of islets and reefs and rocks. Not shallow water — it is deep, but filled with these sharp steep points, rising out of perhaps forty fathoms. At the end of this foul stretch, where it runs out in a triangle across Ballenas Channel, lies Ballenas Islands where the lighthouse is. The tide runs through this channel at three or four knots — and both inside and outside the island there are horrible tide rips.

I kept in the deep channel next to the shore. There was no perceptible tide — it didn't matter anyway; we were not going very far. But I should have known that it was going to blow from the west, for the clouds overhead were still coming fast from that direction. We were over half-way there when the whole gulf came down on top of us in one vast squall; with two hundred miles of push behind it . . . .

We rounded the point of the bay, just this side of North-West Bay, thinking that we might find shelter in there — but the whole bay was foaming white, and spray was being sent dashing up the cliffs. Then the realization suddenly hit me — why the next bay was called North-West — the wind would be piling in there just as it was in the bay beside us . . . . We had to decide, and decide quickly, what we were going to do. About in line with the point of North-West Bay, and about a mile from where we were, I could see a small, unknown, wooded island. And there was a patch of calm water off its southern end. It was too rough even to think of looking at a chart, but that patch might just enable us to ride out the storm.

We headed towards it. There was a crazy black spar-buoy, seventy yards to seawards of us. I knew that I shouldn't be on the inside of it, but I could not possibly go out into that tide rip. The wind would swoop down on top of the buoy and press it flat on the water and the white spray would foam over it. I had to go fairly close to it, for there were unmarked dangers off the point inside us.

The glass in front of me was completely obscured with the spray that struck the bow and dashed over us. On the shore side of the black buoy the waves were not so very high — they hadn't had time yet. It was the force of the wind that made a fine spray, three or four feet high, all over the face of the water. I had to put my head out through the canvas curtain to see anything — and my hair and face streamed water.

"We are almost there, Mummy," Jan called. She kept a small patch of glass clear on her side, with a rag. There was a sheltering wing of heavy kelp shielding the windward side of the little cove we were heading for. I could see a bit of beach up at the end, so I should be able to anchor. Every other place was just a rocky shore of cliffs.

Then the sudden calm — almost breath-taking — and we were in shelter. I edged in. Jan and Peter went on deck, and between the two of them managed to slide the anchor rope through the chock and ease the anchor down.

"Pheeew!" echoed John, as I sank down on one of the bunks and tried to towel some of the wet off me.

"That was pretty rough, wasn't it?" said Peter, jumping in off the deck.

I pulled the chart out from behind the steering wheel. We had been too busy trying to see where we were going to bother with a chart that tried to tell us where we *should* go.

"Jan, just look at all the dangers inside that black buoy that we practically shook hands with!" They all had to see the dangers. Just what was the name of this little island we had found — a little island I had not known was there. Heavens! there it was, marked quite plainly — "Mistaken Island."

"Why 'Mistaken'?" asked Jan, looking over my shoulder.

"Perhaps it's going to disappear at high tide," I suggested.

"I'm going to watch that tide like anything!" said John.

"Sillies!" said Peter. "Look at the trees."

I looked around the little cove we were in, and asked Jan what depth she got when she anchored.

"Only about six feet."

I stared at her . . . there was going to be a zero tide in the night. We weren't more than two boat-lengths now from the edge of the kelp, past which the wind and the waves roared . . . . The cove was

127

so small that it didn't even show on the chart. The wind might go down, and again it mightn't. Well, probably someone knew why they had called it "Mistaken" — and probably we would know why, before we left.

While I got ready some very late lunch the children ran across to the north-east end of the island to look at the waves. They came back, blown to bits, and said the waves were terrific. After lunch I left them to tidy up, and I went across to have a look myself. They were terrific . . . and the outlook for the night was dim.

It was when I was on my way back that I discovered we were not alone on the island. I had climbed up on top of a rocky rib that flanked the east side of the cove. Some movement in among the trees caught my eye: I thought it might be a deer. There again . . . and I saw them. Standing waist-deep in the salal, surrounded by half a dozen goats and young kids, stood Robinson Crusoe. They were all standing up on their tiptoes — peering through the trees at our boat . . . .

"Hello, there!" I called.

The man immediately ducked down in the salal, and they all snaked hurriedly off.

"Come back and see us after supper," I shouted.

No answer. He had to cross an open space there. I don't think he realized that I could still see him — Robinson Crusoe had not yet learned to make his clothes out of goat skins — he just didn't wear any. He looked awfully dark, creeping through the jungle. What were we marooned with? And what had I asked to come and see us after supper?

I told the children about Robinson Crusoe and the goats. They were intrigued, and kept sweeping the woods with the binoculars, but they refused to go ashore again unless I went with them.

I took the pike pole off the cabin top, and with Peter and John rowing, I began to sound the cove and plan for the night which was beginning to look inevitable. The dinghy was tied up astern at the end of the long rope — I don't think anyone could have rowed against that wind; at times it swept in withering squalls across the end of the kelp bed.

I had hoped that the bed of the cove might slope steeply. It didn't — it hardly dropped at all for the first ten yards. There were only ten feet under the stern of the boat now. The water might rise another two or three feet on the end of this tide — but it was going to drop fourteen feet in the night . . . . I decided on a plan, hauled in the dinghy, carried a stern anchor out as far as I dared, and let it down. There were roughly about fifteen feet of water there — that left three feet during the night, if the anchor didn't drag when I pulled the boat out to it.

Then I lifted the bow anchor into the dinghy, rowed farther into the cove, and firmly wedged the anchor behind a big rock. If I pulled the boat between the two anchors during the night, I should be able to keep her off the bottom — always supposing I could keep her out of the wind.

After supper I ran the engine for a while. If my plan for the night didn't work, I could slip both anchors and work along the rocky shore to our left, as far as the calm area extended, which wasn't very far. However, with the engine idling out of gear most of the time, I should be able to linger there for a couple of hours at low water. The chart showed quite a big cove just beyond that — but it was evidently dry at low tide, and some way beyond as well. There was certainly no *better* hole.

We made up the bunks, then went on shore and lighted a fire.

"Mummy," whispered Peter, "he's there." Crusoe was standing at the edge of the trees, looking at us.

"Come on down," I said, still not quite sure what was coming. Very slowly he approached and sat on a rock near us; but he didn't say anything until I asked a direct question.

"What about this cove for the night?" I said.

"Not very good."

"What about the cove farther round?" I pointed.

"My cove. No good."

"Why?" I asked.

"All mud." He shook his head sadly.

"You mean the whole island has no shelter?"

He nodded . . . very, very sadly.

"Is there any fresh water?"

Evidently not. I finally extracted from him that he had to row over to North-West Bay for water and provisions once a week. He was looking after a mink ranch on the north-west end of the island. He caught fish to feed the mink with. And if he didn't get any fish, he killed a kid for them.

I offered him a cigarette, and he took it so eagerly that I gave him the rest of the package and suggested that he go home now before it got dark. He said "Yes," and got to his feet. When he reached the top of the cove he gave a strange little chirruping call, and in seconds the goats and kids appeared and grouped around him. Then they all drifted off into the trees.

"Mummy!" said Jan, "how could you go on talking to him? What is the matter with him?"

"I'm not sure, perhaps just bushed — too much alone. Let's get to bed."

The youngsters were soon quietly asleep. I had been off-hand about the night, and they seemed assured that there would be no trouble. I didn't undress, and sat there wearing my sleeping bag to keep warm. A westerly, in summer time, either goes down with the sun — or else pauses and then blows with renewed vigour. This one hadn't even bothered with the pause.

The sky was clear, the stars were out, and later there should be a moon to light things up. At the moment I couldn't see anything except the night life in the water that stirred up the multitudinous phosphorescent specks of plankton that filled the sea.

I settled down to a routine — up on the deck forward, sound with the pike pole . . . let out rope if necessary. Back to the after-deck, sound . . . pull in slack. My hands dripped luminous jewels from their finger-tips — jewels that exploded in soft flashes as they hit the sea. The whole disturbed anchor rope looked like a shining serpent, writhing off into the twinkling void. Down below there, bigger flashes darted after smaller flashes; and smaller flashes darted after still smaller ones. Then the moon came up — and the night life of the fishes and plankton became obscured.

More line out — more line in. We were getting closer and closer to the outer edge of the calm area; and the wind, but not the waves, was beginning to push us around a little. Just how long can one night be?

We have a book by Dunsany on board — a collection of stories. In the first one, "Idling down the River Yan," when the hour of prayer sounds, and all the men on deck fall on their knees to pray to their various gods, he doesn't quite like to pray to his jealous God, in the midst of all these strange gods. So he prays to a very old God — one who hasn't been prayed to for a long time.

I think this ancient idea of having special gods for special things was very sound. Some religions have special saints who, I expect, look after the practical end of things. Tonight, for instance, I feel the need of a specialized deity — one experienced in nautical matters. The west coast Indians had various gods they prayed to for certain things. Ha-we-im, for good hunting; Kwa-yetsim, to cure the sick — much used by the medicine men. And in bad or dangerous weather at sea they prayed to a Queen Hakoom, who lived above or beyond the seas. They would shout to her, asking her to cause the waves to calm down. They probably still shout to her in times of stress . . . like tonight. I don't think I would care to intrude — much less shout, if that is necessary. But a small prayer to that very old God — the one that hasn't been prayed to for a long time — no one could object to that. This old God must miss the prayers he no longer gets — and might be glad to lend a hand. I feel a gentle but definite jar through the boat. I do not need to be told what it is — "Old God, get busy!"

I scrambled out on deck and grabbed the pike pole — my extra weight up in the bow didn't help. I loosened the line, then leant on the pole and pushed . . . and fortunately oozed her off.

At least the bottom was either mud or sand. And we were undoubtedly getting some back swell. I sounded at the stern — there were only three feet there now, and we drew two and a half. I had left it too late to think of backing out — one rock, and we would be finished. I couldn't take up any more slack in the stern line — I would have to let her bump a bit on the mud, up in the bow . . . .

I wiped my cold wet hands and bundled the sleeping bag closer round me. It was one-thirty — the tide must be low at two or thereabouts. The moon was behind clouds, and it was dark. Once more the crests of the waves were throwing the luminous glow on ahead of them.

That old god must have been out of practice — or perhaps, very wise. For dawn was all about me when I woke at four o'clock — the eastern sky lighting up in long streaks of gold. There had been no need for me to keep awake; everything was quiet, and the wind had blown itself out, or else gone to other seas. I hastily slackened the stern line, and burrowed back into my bag.

131

Trouble

T WAS ONE OF THOSE SUDDEN UNPLANNED THINGS. I had called in to see some friends of mine on my way up from Vancouver, late in September. The weather had been perfect and I was reluctant to cross the gulf for home and settle down for the winter. Settling down meant school every day from nine to one around the dining room table; sawing wood and doing various other outside jobs in the afternoon. And although it had nothing whatever to do with settling down, and couldn't possibly be connected with, nor blamed on it — it meant the beginning of the rainy weather. British Columbia winters, although mild, are definitely rainy. Most of the year's rain falls in the four winter months. So if September was fine, we deliberately stayed on the other side of the gulf. We knew from past experience that once on our own side the pull of Little House would be too strong for us — we would just rush to the settling down.

So we sat on the beach with these friends, happy and contented, telling them all about our summer trip. Then we talked about Princess Louisa, and they said that some day they must see it. And I said, how about taking a quick trip up there now? I had only the two boys on board then, so there was plenty of room. It took them just ten minutes to decide, and by lunch time they and their two children were on board with us and we were off. Some friends are so satisfactory. You may not agree with them in everything or anything, but it doesn't matter. You like each other just as you are. It is the contact and rubbing up against other ideas that is stimulating and rewarding.

We had left too late in the day to get the whole way up Jervis that night. But we found a little corner in Goliath Bay, just out of Agamemnon Channel, where they could put up their tent.

The weather was still sunny the next morning, but we could see the clouds massing round the peaks to the north-east. There was no wind, which was very nice, but the farther we pushed our way into the mountains, the lower the clouds settled.

By the time we reached the entrance to Louisa it had begun to drizzle, and we had to tie up for a while until the tide turned to let us through.

As we sat with the mountains all glooming round us, I told them of the effects that Louisa Inlet had on some people: such a strong feeling of claustrophobia that they would not stay in over night. Fishermen have told me that nothing would induce them to tie up in Louisa in the winter time, on account of the rock slides and avalanches.

One man told a tale of going through the entrance just before dark one winter's afternoon, to get out of the wind that was blowing hard down from the head of Jervis. In the inlet you can't anchor out in the middle, it is too deep. So you can't avoid being near the cliffs. He had tied his boat to a snag on the shore of the rock-flat just inside the entrance. Then he put out a stern anchor to hold him off the shore.

Around ten o'clock the wind rose to a gale — accompanied at times by thunder and lightning. He was reasonably protected from the wind where he was, until the williwaws started blowing down on him from above. These winds can blow over and down from the top of the mountains with enough force to break a deck in.

He was settling down for a night's watch, not attempting to go to bed, when the first avalanche came, soon followed by others. He could hear the great shock and splash of them above the roar of the wind. Then the lightning got brighter and showed up what before he had not been able to see . . . .

An avalanche of mixed snow and rock fell right beside him, covering the boat with salt spray and snow. Giving his boat up for lost, he turned to his own survival. Frantically, he pulled the boat closer to the shore by the bowline. He jumped . . . missed by a couple of feet. Waist deep in the freezing water he clawed his way up the slippery rocks, losing his flashlight somewhere in the effort.

Now in the pitch dark, by each flash of lightning, head down into the wind, he made his way in spurts across the rock-flat to the Jervis Inlet end of the rapids, where an old German had a cabin. Finally he made his pounding heard above the noise of the storm, and stumbled into old Casper's cabin. Old Casper stood up there holding up a candle, his hair standing straight up on end; his ten cats crowding around him — equally electrified. The candle blew out, and the fisherman said you could see the electricity

133

playing all round them. In the morning they found the boat adrift, but still floating, with her cabin completely flat under a fall of rock and snow.

I was eyeing the cliffs too, when I finished the story. Then the tide turned and we went through. I had wanted them to see Louisa at its best, and all I could show them was the dim outline of where the high lip of the cliffs ended and the sky began. But extra waterfalls had started up all along the mile-high cliffs, and hung like white ribbons trailing in the water.

We rounded the overhanging cliff, and there were the big falls throwing themselves twice the distance usual in the summer. And the roar came out to meet us soon after we turned the cape.

It was raining harder now and the whole place was closing in. Trapper's Rock was out of the question. I didn't know if the Man from California would still be there. But even if he weren't, he had a big woodshed that would hold the over-flow from the boat for one night.

He was there — and there had been no boats in for two weeks. If we waited an extra day and gave him a chance to pack up for the winter, he would go down with us. He insisted on our all staying up at the cabin with him, so we carted up our sleeping bags and our box of provisions and settled down happily in front of the big fireplace. The great fall shouted and moaned. Every now and then there would be a heavy thud, which our host said was when the waterfall threw boulders out ahead of it.

It was the next day after lunch that John fell over the balcony that ran across in front of the upstairs bedrooms above the fireplace. We were busy washing up in the kitchen, so nobody knows just what did happen. He and the other children were playing around upstairs and generally fooling. He probably fell on the floor as someone chased him, and slid through under the one high rail down onto the floor below.

There was that horrible soft thud, and a shout from above. We all knew exactly what it was .... I suppose we all had the same desperate selfish wish, "Oh, not mine?" as we crowded into the room.

John lay on the floor, gasping for breath .... He had just missed the heavy log arm of the end of the chesterfield. A minute later, while I was still not daring to move him, he sat up and moved each arm. "Not broken," he gasped. Then he looked up at the antlers above the fireplace, "Lucky I missed those!" Then he was violently sick . . . bringing up a certain amount of blood as well.

We carried him upstairs and got him into bed. He continued to be sick every half-hour — and always there were traces of blood. Then I suddenly realized that the vomiting could very well be just from shock with a highly strung child. So I started filling him up with corn syrup. In a couple of hours that took effect and he fell asleep. I began to wonder then if he had really landed on his head and had a slight concussion . . . .

I tiptoed out and crept downstairs. I drank a good stiff drink, and then we discussed what it was best to do. It was pouring rain outside and blowing hard — and the falls were roaring and prophesying doom. We were sixty miles from a doctor and help, and in this wind it would be a very rough trip down.

They said it was up to me — and I decided that it would be better just to keep him in bed for another day. If more serious symptoms appeared, and the wind did not abate, then we would have to think of fighting our way down, or one of the men might go in my boat and come back with the doctor in a bigger boat. We could always change our minds, but now we would wait and see.

I crept up every half-hour to look at John, and still he slept — moaning a little whenever he moved. He woke up later and I gave him more syrup. One thing that worried me was the way he kept his head turned sideways, and pressed hard against his right shoulder.

At ten o'clock he was feverish . . . . He had a restless night, moaning and talking in his sleep. I was up every hour with him — bathing his hands and face, coaxing down a little more syrup, worrying about his head on his shoulder. Then about four in the morning he must have slept more quietly, for I fell asleep too and it was eight o'clock before we woke up. He no longer seemed to be feverish and I breathed more easily. I persuaded him to try to eat some breakfast. But he wanted very little.

It was still blowing and raining, and I could see no reason for changing the plan of waiting until the next day. He felt better after eating some lunch, and was interested in my reading to him. Then everybody came up to see him and looked at his crooked head against his shoulder. He wouldn't let anyone touch it, and all we

135

could get out of him was that he liked it that way.

We had everything packed and ready to leave the next day, though with John obviously better we decided to wait until the wind dropped. The tide at the entrance would be slack at nine.

There was no wind in the morning, and although it was dull, the rain had stopped. John ate his breakfast, and we carried him down to the boat and rolled him up in blankets on one of the bunks. We were relieved on rounding Patrick Point to find that all was quiet in the main part of the inlet. No one was anxious to face a rough sea all day with a sick child.

There is a little hospital at Pender Harbour, and we made straight for it as soon as we anchored, only to find that the doctor was away and would not be back for a week.

So we parted with the Man from California and went on down to Thormanby Island, where a doctor I knew had a summer cottage. The doctor's wife was there, but he was down in Vancouver.

It blew again the next day and I couldn't get my friends back to their home — twenty-five miles farther down the coast . . . . It was hard to keep John quiet on a crowded boat, and our food was running short. The caretaker on the island said that he could flag the weekly boat, which should be in at five o'clock, though we couldn't count on the time. Our friends decided that it would be better for them to go home by the boat and leave me free to cross the gulf as soon as the weather cleared.

The boat didn't whistle until after seven — we piled into the dinghy and rowed out in the dark. The great menacing steamer lurched up against the anchored float — all the bay had as a wharf. They threw a rope down to us — and a gang plank was finally fixed at a precarious angle and my friends clambered on board. It was not until the men at the boat end of the rope yelled at me two or three times that I realized I was supposed to cast off the steamer. I finally managed to free her and she faded away, leaving me alone on a spinning raft with all my sense of direction gone.

I waited until the raft settled down in its normal position and groped my way to the dinghy. I had left my flashlight on board with the boys, in case they might be nervous alone there.

I tried to get straight back to the boat — but it was so dark I might have been going in circles. Then I saw the blink-blink-blink of a little light off in the distance. It could be in quite the wrong direction, but I thought it was probably Peter trying to see if I were coming — so I rowed towards it. After ten minutes more rowing, I hailed . . . and Peter shouted in reply.

"Did you see our S O S?" they asked when I got within talking distance. "We didn't like being marooned."

It was blowing again the next day, and I felt that we were never going to get home. The day after, it was too unsettled to start in the morning. But after lunch it was quiet. I decided to start and get as far as Lasqueti Island for the night. It was a longer way, but at least we should be half-way across the gulf.

The little hole on the south-east end of Lasqueti is very small and sometimes quite hard to find. There is a small float to tie up to, but no room to anchor. There were two fish-boats already there when we arrived. They made room for us and helped us tie up. They thought if we left at six in the morning we could get across before anything very much blew up.

If I hadn't been so anxious to get home to find out why John's head was on crooked, I don't suppose I would have left. It wasn't actually blowing at six, but it looked as though it was going to. A west wind doesn't usually start up until around nine or later. This one began at seven. It waited until we were half-way across. The tide was flooding, and in the stretch between the Ballenas and Lasqueti, wind against tide creates a nasty tide rip which gets worse as you near the other side. So I had to turn down the gulf with the wind more on our tail, steering for the little group of islands where the fishermen had showed us the emergency anchorage.

A following sea is the most upsetting to be in. John was sick again, and all my fears came crowding back. I couldn't have put his life jacket on over that head either. Peter, I could see, didn't like it much, and I couldn't produce a whistle to calm their fears. I couldn't leave the wheel to help John, and it wasn't safe to let him lean over the edge. Peter gave him a tin and he had to manage by himself.

In about another hour we were out of the rip. It was blowing harder, but with a different kind of wave. Then down the narrow passage, and finally into that blessed little haven.

The wind shimmered across the water in sudden sweeps, but

there was no sea. We anchored and made ourselves a good break-fast, and with the heat from the stove got all warm and dry again. John felt better and the sun came out.

It was blowing very hard now from the west, and there was no question of going on until the wind dropped. We landed on one of the low islands that compose the group — very low with such a high tide. The whole gulf was one vast expanse of white caps — racing and galloping along. We were so close to the surface that it made you feel that the island was doing the rocking.

We got home the next day after lunch and I raced John right over to the doctor before we even changed. The doctor asked a lot of questions and looked at his head and felt around his shoulder. Then he said to John, "It's all right, old chap, you can lift your head up now — it won't hurt any more."

John warily lifted his head up straight. "Why it's all better," he smiled. "It doesn't hurt now, isn't that good!"

"He had a broken collar-bone," the doctor explained, "and he has been holding himself the only way it didn't hurt — a doctor couldn't have done any more for him." Then he made me feel the ridge of bone that had already built up around the fracture. No need now for even a sling. The blood, he explained, had probably been a broken blood-vessel. The vomiting, certainly shock, and I had done the right thing to stop it.

Well . . . ! We were not used to those kind of troubles. If we had had more of them, I suppose, I wouldn't have been so upset.

A Whale . . . Named Henry

HE "COAST PILOT" AT TIMES EITHER TERRIFIES US OR else gets us into trouble. Quite naturally, I suppose; for they have big vessels in mind — and what does or doesn't do for a big vessel isn't always right for the little boat. That is where the local inhabitants are a help. One of them says to us: "Oh, you don't have to do that — you can take a short cut. See that island? Follow it down until you come to the old sawmill. Then line the sawmill up with the three maples on the low point, about a mile down on the opposite shore. Follow that line — and it will lead you through the reefs and kelp. After you reach the maples, it's all clear. Save you about five miles, and you won't have to wait for slack at the narrows."

We follow instructions — it doesn't look anything like a mill, but there are squared timbers on the ground and the remains of a roof. Then we look along the far shore, until off in the distance we spot the three maples. We steer across on the long angle . . . . Someone shouts "Rocks!" but they are to one side and not on the line. If we follow instructions and don't question them, we never get into trouble in using the local short cuts.

The *Coast Pilot*, speaking of Sechelt Inlet, says: "Three miles within its entrance, it contracts to a breadth of less than one-third of a mile, and is partially choked with rocks and small islands which prevent in great measure the free ingress and egress of the tide, causing the most furious and dangerous rapids, the roar of which can be heard for several miles." These rapids, whose maximum velocity is from ten to twelve knots, "prevent any boat from entering the inlet except for very short periods at slack water." Then it adds that "It would be hazardous for any boat, except a very small one, to enter at any time."

Well, we were a very small boat, thoroughly terrified by the Pilot book, and we were creeping cautiously along on the far side — listening for the roar. When we heard it, we supposed that we should have to wait for it to stop, and then we would get through.

"Just like Henry," breathed Peter and John, all excited. Someone, three or four years ago, had told me a true story about a blackfish or killer whale that had gone through Skookumchuck Rapids into the inlet, and couldn't find his way out again. He was evidently in there for a couple of years. All the tugboat men knew him. When they tooted their whistles the whale always appeared, hoping they would show him the way out.

Only last winter Peter and John and I had been sitting in front of the big fireplace trying to think of a book to read aloud. Books to read aloud are much harder to find than just books to read. Finally, I suggested that if the three of us put our heads together, we should be able to write one for ourselves. Peter and John took this literally and their heads came *bang* — against mine. Peter shouted, "Contact!" and John said, "Sparks!" and up came, of all things, a blackfish.

I sat there holding my head. What on earth had made me think of a blackfish, which is just a local name for a killer whale? The only one I had ever given a second thought to was of course the one that had gone through the Skookumchuck and couldn't find his way out again — it always rather intrigued me. But who would ever try to write a story about a whale!

I had to stop thinking. Peter kept asking, "What have you got?" And John, very eagerly, "What did you see?" and I was feeling more and more reluctant to tell them. I finally suggested that we try it again, just to make sure, and then I would tell them.

"Well, we'll do it harder this time," warned Peter. And they did.

"Contact!" cried Peter, expectantly.

"Sparks!" said John, in a very deep voice, as though he thought the stronger the sparks, the better the results.

And there again — only worse — much more definite. In words — "Up the coast there lived a whale — named Henry."

So, in despair, I had to tell them. There was a pause, and John, always ready to make the best of a thing like that, cried excitedly, "And he could be sick and throw up 'amber-grease' and we could find it!"

And Peter said scornfully, "Don't be silly, he wouldn't do that. And anyway, this is to be a story, and he's going to have a'ventures."

Peter and John finally went to bed, and I sat there alone — perfectly miserable, with a whale — named Henry — on my hands. I thought of trying to get rid of him, but it was too late for that — I even knew what he looked like. Beyond that I knew nothing; and I stuck at that point for ages. Then, one night, when there was still nothing to read, John started to cry . . . . "Well, put the period at the end," he sobbed; "that will be *something* anyway."

So, for some time, there was a big, round, black period, patiently waiting on the last page — and John felt a little happier.

I had never even been in Sechelt Inlet — but with the aid of a chart, the *Coast Pilot*, and a good deal of imagination, Henry finally reached the big black period — and the tale was ended. And this was the story of Henry, the Whale . . . .

"Phuph..e..e..w!" blew Henry in disgust as he just missed a salmon that sprang out of his way.

"Phuph..e..e..w!" blew Henry in alarm when he tried to swim back the way he had come. He didn't seem to be making any headway at all. Henry tried again and again but a whirlpool sprang at him and spun him round and round. Then it sucked him down . . . down . . . round . . . faster and faster. Then up he was thrown to the surface and he blew out his breath with a roar.

The Skookumchuck rapids tossed him out on to a jagged point of rock and the strong waters pulled and tore at him. They tossed him along and then threw him up into the quiet inland arm of the sea. He lay bruised and bleeding.

A salmon rose out of the water and seeing him darted away in fright. He swam up and down the bays and inlets spreading fear among the other fish telling them about the big killer whale in the arm.

"What!" shrieked a seal who was about to make a meal of the salmon but closed his mouth in time. "A whale in the inlet? How terrible!"

Henry lay motionless in a great bed of kelp — thirty feet of black and white misery. He lay for three days without stirring. Just when the crab and the rock cod who lived there were working on how long one whale, thirty feet by eight feet, by six feet would live — Henry moved his tail. Not very much, but he could feel it all the way up to his head.

"Oooooooh!" he groaned.

Everything in the kelp bed scuttled for their lives except the crab — who had done the most work on the problem and waited to see what the answer would be. However, Henry moved his tail again and it wasn't quite so bad this time. He tried moving his eyes next and found that he could still see. He tried thinking. What had happened? Then he suddenly felt very guilty remembering his mother saying over and over, "Keep away from the Skookum-chuck rapids. If you ever have to go in, wait for slack tide to come out again." Henry remembered it all now but he had been diving and rolling along the inlet when a great school of salmon had suddenly appeared. He was so excited that he had followed them, forgetting everything else (and not even noticing that they were heading for the Skookumchuck). Henry groaned again and the

141

crab looked expectant.

The next day Henry felt so much better he decided he would look for the way out. When he began moving about he realized he was quite hungry. In a couple of great gulps Henry swallowed all the inhabitants around him — including the crab whose arithmetic didn't interest him at all.

"That feels better!" sighed Henry and away he swam. But no matter which way he turned he bumped into a cliff. "This is getting tiresome. I'll have to ask somebody."

Henry spied a seal, but the seal saw him first and swam off in a flurry.

"Hi there," he called seeing a school of salmon. But they leapt out of the water and continued leaping until they were out of sight. "Nasty rude things!" Growling and grumbling to himself Henry sank into the depths to try and think what to do next.

"Well," yawned a voice from somewhere, "If you have rested long enough I wish you would get off my rock, I want to catch my supper."

Henry's jaw dropped. The voice sounded as much under him as any place else. He raised himself slightly and tried to look underneath — but it was very hard to see. "Where are you anyway?"

"Right here on the rock beside you," said the voice.

"I don't know what you are and I still can't see you."

"Look harder," chuckled the voice. Henry stared and stared. Then right there on the rock, where Henry was sure it wasn't, was a large red octopus with its long arm coiled about itself. As Henry stared it slowly faded out of sight again.

"What do you think of that?" asked the voice.

"Stupid," said Henry crossly. Then from nothing came a cloud of dirty black water and something reached out and pulled his nose.

"You horrid miserable jellyfish," raged Henry swishing his tail around and flattening everything. "I'll squash you for that."

He banged down on the rock and stayed there, wondering if you could eat what you couldn't see — and what it would taste like if you could. A school of rock cod came swimming by and goggled at a stone-grey octopus arm waving at them from a crack in the rock upon which Henry was sitting so hopefully. They giggled nervously and Henry said, "Hush! I've just squashed an octopus and I'm listening." The cod rushed off in a frenzy at the idea of an octopus teasing a thirty-foot whale.

Henry began to tire of sitting on what he could neither see nor feel and he just had to get up for more air, so he gave an especially hard squash and shot to the surface. Then he remembered suddenly that he had gone down there in the first place to think. Seeing a rocky island ahead he eyed it with satisfaction. "Just the place for a think," he said.

After a good long think Henry decided that the best way to find the way out was to look for the roar first. Then he would know he was at the Skookumchuck and when the roar stopped and he could see the green stain on the white rock the tide would be slack and he would swim through. Simple. Henry was very pleased with himself.

"Now," said Henry, "All I have to do is to swim along the surface until I hear the roar. If I keep the cliffs on my left side I won't get confused." Every cliff Henry rounded he would listen carefully. It grew dark and still Henry swam on. The cliffs grew dark and tall and Henry swam on watching the stars. A cold grey light began to spread over everything. Seagulls looked pale against the silvery light. Henry could make out a deep bay just ahead of him and decided that it would make a good place for breakfast. The whole bay tossed and heaved with commotion and Henry's cavernous mouth devoured everything in sight.

As Henry swam out of the bay he saw a white goat come down on a point of land. It stood there and made the kind of noises goats make. Henry stared. This was something new. The goat came down to look at Henry who was new to him too. Whatever it was the goat decided, Henry would be company, and he jumped and hopped over the rocks alongside of him. Whenever Henry stopped the goat would stop, his head, with its ridiculous beard, tilted to one side. Henry decided he didn't like it and tried blowing at it. But that seemed a waste of time as the goat seemed to enjoy it.

"I'll race and leave it behind," decided Henry. So away he tore with the goat following and soon left it behind. Henry raced on. Then suddenly — oh no, not another one! This time Henry wasn't waiting to see if it would follow but tore past it at full speed. The goat had time only to turn his head as Henry raced by. Every mile

or so was a narrow channel and great frowning heights and then
— another goat . . . ! They were getting as thick as minnows.
Henry put on an extra spurt.

Another goat! Henry blinked. Something *was* wrong. He was
beginning to feel quite queer. Henry stopped with a lurch and the
whole world with the goat standing on top went round and round
and round. Henry felt very sick.

An angry kingfisher bird spluttered at him from a dead branch.
"Look here, what are you racing around and around our island
for?"

Henry stared. "Island?"

"Yes island. You've been around it half a dozen times now and
it's becoming quite upsetting."

"Oh dear," sighed Henry, "I shall have to start all over again."

Evening came calm and cool and peaceful and Henry settled
down to a steady roll. Suddenly right in his path he met Timothy.
Timothy opened his mouth and squawked at him. He was a very
young seagull and "Squaaaawk," said Timothy again more in-
sistently.

Henry was so astonished that he could only stare. Things —
especially small things — didn't usually squawk at him. Then as
he stared, Timothy opened his mouth again and held it open —
quite plainly telling him that he expected Henry to fill it.

This really was embarrassing. How could a whale feed a bird?
Timothy looked at him with bright and fearless eyes. Henry
wiggled his tail.

"Look here," he protested. "What's the matter with you —
don't you realize what I am? Why aren't you flying anyway?"

"Can't," answered Timothy, "I have a broken wing."

Henry looked. One soft grey wing had been broken just above
the second joint. "A man mended it for me but it's still not good."
It had been carefully set with three matches and bound with a
piece of fishing twine.

"Hmmm," said Henry trying to think of something to distract
the bird so it would forget about being hungry. "What's your
name?"

"The man that fixed my wing called me Timothy."

"Timothy! Why did he call you that?"

"Because my toes are pink."

"Oh," said Henry, eyeing him nervously, and Timothy opened his mouth wide and squawked.

"I — I say," protested Henry desperately, "I haven't got anything to eat and I wouldn't know how to feed you if I had."

"Couldn't you catch me even one little fish?" pleaded Timothy.

And that is where Henry made his first mistake. He said alright rather ungraciously and then dived and presently appeared with a nice grilse in his mouth which he put in front of Timothy and hastily backed away. Timothy was quite capable of eating it himself and when he had finished and had rinsed his beak and ruffled his feathers as well as he could with the broken wing, he turned confidently to Henry and asked, "Well, what shall we do now?"

That was when Henry made his second mistake. He stammered, "Whaaat?" He tried to mend matters when the seagull repeated the question by saying he couldn't do anything as he was looking for a way out.

"Way out of what?" asked the seagull.

"The way out of this inlet, of course," said Henry gloomily.

"Why I've often been out of here," said Timothy. Henry turned and stared at him. "Often been out," repeated the seagull, nodding his head, "Often, often."

"And you'll show me?" asked Henry eagerly.

Timothy said he would but tomorrow, not tonight as he was sleepy and without even bothering to say goodnight, tucked his head under his good wing and went to sleep bobbing gently on the water.

Henry was left wondering if it were safe to trust a seagull who was called Timothy because his feet were pink but since there was nothing he could do about it anyway he decided that he would go to sleep too.

It was quite light when Henry woke up the next morning — or rather was wakened up. "Squaaawk," said a voice suddenly in his ear. Then he remembered.

"I wish you wouldn't do that before I'm awake," grumbled Henry.

But Timothy wasn't intimidated and just opened his mouth wider. Henry knew what was expected of him and grumpily told Timothy to stay where he was and dove out of sight. It took some time to find Timothy's breakfast since he decided to eat his own while he was down there. It takes a lot to fill up a killer whale. Finally Henry felt satisfied and seeing a small grilse he said, "Just the thing for Timothy," and took it carefully in his teeth.

He exploded through the surface but there was no sign of one small seagull. He was afraid he had come rather a long way. He tried calling the bird but it didn't come out very well with the fish in his teeth. He tried blowing hoping that might attract his attention but he couldn't give a decent blow either. "Timothy," he called and out shot the grilse. Before the last echo of Henry's shout died away the little fish was safely hidden at the bottom of the sea.

"Now he's made me lose his breakfast," grumbled Henry irritably looking all about him. "Perhaps I've swallowed him," he thought hopefully and gulped a couple of times to see if he could feel anything half way up or half way down.

"Squaaawk," said a voice right beside him. Henry wheeled and there was Timothy sitting with his mouth open and eyes shut.

When Henry had replaced the bird's breakfast and he had rinsed off his beak he said, "Well, come along and I'll show you the way out now."

It wasn't long before Timothy was exhausted paddling along trying to keep up with Henry. "You'll have to give me a ride."

"Ride," exclaimed Henry. This was an indignity to end all indignities. Pat-pat-pat, cold pink toes pattered up his back accompanied by much squawking and fluttering for Henry was very slippery.

Henry gave a cautious roll forward and Timothy slid squawking down his back. Just as he reached Henry's blow-hole Henry let out his breath and up shot Timothy into the air.

"Beast," spluttered the bird as he flopped into the water with a splash.

"Sorry," said Henry cheerfully, "It wasn't my fault."

"Of course it was your fault. Who ever heard of anyone having waterfalls in the top of their head anyway?"

"You'd better swim then," said Henry.

"I won't," said Timothy.

"Well don't. I'll find my own way out." Henry blew savagely and decided to teach Timothy a lesson and tore round and round making huge waves. Up and down bobbed Timothy not making a peep.

"Alright," shouted Henry, "You can ride."

Timothy decided to try behind Henry's big fin this time and so long as he rolled gently the seagull was able to stay on. Presently Henry felt that something was not right. It was dark now but Henry could feel that the water was getting shallow and still no sign of the way out. He was just about to say as much when there were excited squawks from Timothy.

"I can see it. I can see it. Straight ahead."

Henry went forward cautiously trying to see in the darkness, but as far as he could see, trees loomed in an unbroken circle against a quiet sky. What was worse, the water was getting shallower and shallower. Then he felt weeds tickling his tummy.

"What are you stopping for," shrieked Timothy stamping his cold pink toes.

"Because there isn't enough water," said Henry darkly.

"That doesn't matter, its only fifty yards across here and then we are right out in the open water."

"Fifty yards of what?"

"Sand," shrieked Timothy. "Nice soft sand."

So that's what soft pink toes led to — nice soft sand. He might have known. "Get off my back," thundered Henry and Timothy got off. "Now go on."

Timothy started off obediently but looking back over his shoulder in a bewildered way he asked, "But aren't you coming too?"

"I — can't — swim — in — sand!"

"Oh." And in the darkness Timothy heard a big watery sob, "Shall we try again," he said in a little wee voice.

Gently Henry backed out of the shallow water. In the dark he turned slowly around and moved ahead. Dark outlines of cliffs drifted past and then suddenly they seemed right on top of them. Henry raised himself out of the water to look. Along the shore the water was making soft gurgling noises, climbing up the stones as far as it could reach, then suck-suck, as it drew back again. Against Henry's sides it rippled, lip-lip-lip. Hurry, hurry, lapped the impatient ripples. Gurgle, gurgle, said the little eddies. Hurry, hurry, louder and louder, faster and faster. Henry lay there wondering and thinking. Then everything kept getting louder and louder and stronger and more insistent.

"It's certainly making enough noise," he was thinking, "roaring like anything. Roaring!" he jumped. Of course it was roaring. "Timothy," he bellowed, "jump off. It's the Skookumchuck and I have to hurry while the tide is slack. If you stay on you will get drowned. I've found it. I've found the way out. Jump off. Goodbye. I'll see you on the other side."

Poor Timothy was quite shaken up but he jumped and paddled to the shore by the light of the moon. He watched Henry move ahead through the whirlpools and ripples that were gentled now.

Henry could feel the roaring waters close behind on his tail. Suddenly he saw the Indian village and he knew he was out and safe.

"Out," he shouted, "Why I'm out! Out, out!"

A little voice back on shore echoed, "Out, out. Henry's out. Ha, ha. Henry's out."

It was after that that we decided to go into the inlet ourselves, and see all the places and things that Henry had. So now, just like Henry, we were trying to find the roar. Suddenly, we heard it — and then we saw the water boiling out from behind the farthest island: The Indian name "Skookumchuck" means "Strong Waters." How smoothly the translation flows, and how the Indian name boils, swirls and roars! We hastily tied up to a private float against the shore. I should have liked to ask some of the local people about it — before we tried it, even at slack. But the house on the hill was empty, and no boat lay at the wharf.

We ate our lunch while waiting for the roar to stop. We had just finished, when ahead of us, on our side, we could hear the whine of an approaching outboard engine. The sea there seemed completely choked with kelp and small islands, but out from behind an island came a rowboat with an outboard and one man — without a doubt, a local inhabitant. No one else could have wound through that kelp with his sure feeling. Then into the open he came — straight our way — and tied up at the float.

We were round him in an instant, asking questions. He first asked how much our boat drew. Then told us that we could get through where he had come, at any time and any tide. There was a passage through the kelp, about eight feet wide and four feet deep. We couldn't mistake it — it showed clearly when you got closer. It led right through into the inlet, and nowhere near the rapids.

"But we've *got* to go through the rapids," broke in John, "because Henry did."

"Who is Henry?" the man asked him.

"Henry was a whale," Peter answered. "He went in there, and he couldn't find his way out again."

The man laughed. "I knew that whale, young fellows, but I never thought to ask him what his name was."

We thanked the man, and took off for the kelp-bed — where the ribbon of kelp-free water showed perfectly clearly, just as he had said. Across on the other side the Skookumchuck was still roaring furiously and dangerously — while we slipped in easily through the back entrance. Peter and John were still glooming, because we hadn't gone through where Henry did.

I think it is a mistake to go back to revisit places you have known as a child. They are all changed and shrunken — and you feel lost and lonely. And, I was beginning to suspect — also a mistake to visit a place you knew only from a book. Peter and John were expecting to find this inlet just as they had imagined it — which came to them second hand from what I had imagined. So each of us was going to be disappointed in his own way. A couple of years ago I discovered that Peter thought the government was three men sitting on a green bench. He preferred his version to anything I told him — probably still does for all I know.

I got out the chart and gave Jan the wheel . . . . "Keep to the left, close along the cliff," I said.

"Why?" she asked, as she turned in closer.

"Jan!" said Peter; "don't you *know* that Henry always stuck to his left cliff?"

"There's the little island where he stopped to think," I pointed out. The island satisfied all of us — just about what we had all imagined it to be like. There were the twisted juniper at the edge, the stunted pines on the crest, the moss and stone crop above the high water mark. As Henry said, "Just the place for a think."

One woman editor I sent the story to wrote back to say that "All children don't like personalized animals" — that she herself

149

found it hard to come to grips with Henry.

She was quite mistaken — it was the other way round. I had always imagined that *I* was inside Henry. Now that I was in the inlet I found that I was looking at it entirely from Henry's point of view. If an editor can't get inside a whale, if called upon — it's her own loss — she doesn't have to put it off on the children. Children can imagine anything, and come to grips with it. They have no difficulty whatever in getting inside frogs, rabbits, ducks or anything else — they just take a whale in their stride.

We turned into Narrows Arm, still keeping the cliffs on our left. We could go very close, for there were thirty-five fathoms right off the sheer drop of the cliff. Then the two sides of the arm squeezed together until the cliffs were only about two hundred feet apart. Five-thousand-foot mountains on either side made it seem much narrower. Quite a strong current was swirling through and rushing us along. No wonder Henry thought he had found the way out at this point.

The chart showed the end of the inlet as merging into the Tzoonie River, with four outlets. So I had surmised that it would be shallow with mud flats, and enough fresh water to have a lot of dead jellyfish around — and that was just what we found.

Seagulls were wheeling overhead and screaming at our intrusion. There were lovely, sheer cliffs going up and up and up, in terraces, to over six thousand feet. But boats, like whales, have to think of the water under them. This would be no place to spend the night in — what with mud flats, and the mosquitoes and no-see-ums that the low land behind would breed. So we just took a turn round, with Jan sitting astride the bow as lookout, and got out again as fast as we could . . . and the seagulls jeered and laughed, and settled down on the water again.

There was a little island in the bay just past the narrows — through which we had to fight our way against the current. But the island was steep-to and there was no anchorage. Anyway, we really wanted to spend the night in Storm Bay — where Henry had dropped in for breakfast. So we ate some hardtack and settled for another two hours.

Storm Bay was not really a very good place to spend the night. It was completely open to the west. The wind that blew down Jervis Inlet in the late afternoon and evening was perfectly likely to follow the mountains on into Sechelt Inlet. We had not been in there before, so we didn't know what to expect. There were two little islands just inside the entrance to the bay. By putting out a stern anchor, I strung the boat in between and hoped for a quiet night.

The day had been hot, but now the sun had sunk behind the mountains to the north-west and the air was just pleasantly warm. Slowly the lower hills were taking on that violet hue that would deepen into purple at a later hour.

Dinner over, and the bunks made up, we rowed slowly into the end of the bay. From the cool, dark woods behind, the thrushes called and called with their ringing mounting notes. Back of the beach we found a wooden tub that some fisherman or trapper had sunk into the bank to catch a stream of water trickling over the rock and through the ferns. I leant over and shaded my eyes to see if I could see the bottom of the tub. There on the bottom was a little brown lizard . . . . The lizard, and the water smelling of wet barrel staves, moss and balsam, sent me hurtling back through the years — to a similar though larger barrel, on the cliff path on the way down to the beach at Cacouna, on the lower St. Lawrence below Quebec. There, you had to raise yourself on tiptoes on the wet slippery stones, to drink deep of the cold water that welled over the edge of the barrel . . . . Exactly the same smell to the water — wet wood, moss and fern and balsam. And if you shaded your eyes and looked down at the bottom you almost always saw a little lizard — just like the one at the bottom of this tub in Storm Bay — thousands of miles away.

I told the children about the other barrel, when I was a little girl — so they had to smell the water too, and look at the lizard. John was fascinated by the idea that I could ever have been as little as they were . . . .

"Some day, when you are big, you will find another barrel with a smell like this — and a lizard — and it will bring you right back to Storm Bay," I told them.

Down at Cacouna, as here — the thrushes in the cool woods called and called. Down there, there was another variety as well, that rang down and down — dropping, dropping . . . .

On Sunday mornings, all through the church service in the little white church in the middle of the pine woods — a little church

151

that smelt of scrubbed pine and had hard pine benches to sit on, but little red carpet pads to kneel on — all through the service I listened to the thrushes ringing up — mounting and mounting . . . ringing down . . . dropping and dropping . . . and never heard the service at all.

The water in the bay was quite warm. When it got dark we went in swimming off the boat, so that we could make flying angels. When the water is full of plankton, if you lie on your back and float, and move your arms through the water — first down to your sides, and then up against your head — you make great shining wings.

I climbed back on board with John to watch the other two. Jan started taking big mouthfuls of water and spouting them up in the air — liquid fire that broke and shattered in the air, and fell and splashed. Peter tried it too, but he laughed so much that I had to haul him on board and thump his back — then subdue him with towels.

I finally threatened to pull up the ladder if Jan didn't come out. "I don't care if you do," she said. "I'd like to stay in all night."

Just then a heron let off a shattering "Caaawk" as it swerved over our heads. That was too much for our angel of the spouts, and she climbed up the ladder in a hurry — all wet and shivering.

It was quiet all night. I woke at times to check. Any bay open to a prevailing wind is always an uneasy anchorage. The constellations were slowly wheeling round the Pole star. They had almost made a semi-circle, the last time I woke — and grey light was showing in the east. Then I pulled my sleeping bag over my head, and really slept.

I was wakened by Peter and John arguing whether there had been any fish left in the bay at all — after Henry dropped in for breakfast. I shoo'd them off in the rowboat to look for some, while I had a swim. Even breakfast didn't stop the argument. I pulled the chart out and showed them the island where Henry had found the goat.

"Will the goat still be there?" they demanded.

"Probably," I foolishly said.

Darn Henry anyway! Why on earth had I said that the goat would probably still be there. Peter had the binoculars and was watching the island — and John fought him for them every time

Peter took his eyes from them.

I slowed down a little . . . no use hurrying to meet trouble. Who ever heard of a goat on an island, miles from anywhere — please, oh *please*, let there be a goat . . . .

"I see it!" shrieked Peter, pointing. I grabbed the glasses from him. There, on the point, was a white goat waiting for us.

I sat down. I felt exactly like Saint Theresa — all weak in the knees. Challenged by a guard when she was smuggling forbidden food to starving prisoners, and asked what she had in her basket — "Roses," she said. He pulled off the cloth that covered the basket — and it was full of roses.

That silly goat! It was a wonder we ever got any farther at all that day. It did all the silly things that goats do; and said all the silly things that goats say; and stuck to the children like a leech. It was a young billy, and must have been brought up with children. When they came on board to lunch, it stood on the point, bawling . . . .

It was in the middle of the afternoon when, tired of feeling eternally grateful, I tooted my little whistle and started pulling up the anchor. The youngsters did their best to get back quickly — realizing that my patience was at an end — but the goat jumped into the dinghy too, and they couldn't get him out.

"What will we do?" they wailed, desperate eyes on the anchor. I gave some advice, as well as I could for laughing, and they went on shore again. The goat of course followed. They picked a pile of green leaves for it, and Jan sat beside it while Peter and John got in the dinghy and pushed off a little way. Then, when the goat had a mouthful of green leaves, Jan got a head start — giving a mighty push as she jumped in. Peter pulled on the oars and they were safe. But how that goat bawled, and how the children worried about it!

"How would you like to be a goat, all alone on an island?" demanded Peter. But he didn't take up my offer to leave him behind to keep the goat company. It is bad enough, sometimes, to be cruising with a boat full of children without being pestered with stray characters out of a book.

It is ten miles from Goat Island up to the end of Salmon Arm, which runs off to the north-east from Sechelt Inlet. We fished for our supper on the way, and caught a five-pound salmon — which relieved the tension caused by the lonely goat. Late in the afternoon we made our way slowly alongside the cliff where Henry had waited for so long. Peter and John showed very little interest — they were still discussing the goat. It was I, in spite of myself, who kept looking for the white vein of quartz and the green copper stain — by which Henry had gauged the rise and fall of the tide while he was waiting for the roar of the falls to stop — thinking it was the roar of the Skookumchuck, and the way out. And it was I who kept expecting, and was disappointed not to find, the old Indian village by the falls — "Old-village-by-the-water-that-never-stops."

The end of the arm was not quite as I had expected. I had thought there would be one large, roaring waterfall. It roared all right, but at this season there were three smaller ones, spilling over a wide sweep of smooth sandstone terraces. There were the remains of an old shingle mill, and the flume that had carried water down to turn a generator. Big logs stranded on the sandstone slopes showed what a tremendous volume of water must come over the falls at times. We climbed up the dry sandstone and to our surprise found a large lake — the chart had just shown an unexplored blank.

In the morning we rowed across to the other side of the bay, where we could see a small float held out from the cliff by poles. There was a steep trail leading up through the woods, and high up at the lake level we found a small cabin and an elderly man and his wife. They were caretakers for some fishing club — which kept the lakes stocked with trout — fishing for members only. There were two lakes, the second one much bigger than the first. He said he had an old boat tied up on the lake. We could use it if we would like to row up to the next lake and swim.

We rowed up as far as the second lake, which was about three or four miles long and a mile wide. The two lakes lay in a deep cleft between very high mountains, and must have collected all the drainage from their slopes. The boat was too old and water-logged to row very far.

We drifted along in the shade of the trees, and watched the trout rising to some kind of fly that kept dancing just above the water. I had stooped down to bail the boat again, when I spied a sealed glass jar underneath the "back seat." I picked it up — it was bottled salmon-eggs! Illegal! That old caretaker! What would the fishing club think of that! What did we have on us that we could be illegal with, too? Peter produced a piece of minnow line from his pocket. Jan had a very small safety pin, and I had a lucky ten cent piece with a hole in it. And John, who at first thought he had nothing at all — cut a stick for us.

The ten cent piece made a good lure, although it twisted the line up a bit. An unripe huckleberry looked like a salmon-egg and was not nearly as smelly as those under the seat. We found that you had to have a very quick technique or else these ten-inch trout either bent the pin or slipped off it.

We stopped at four fish. Then wrapped them in cool green fern. When we got back to the landing, I sent the youngsters back by the sandstone terraces with the fish — while I went back by the cabin to thank them for the boat.

"I could have lent you a line," he said, "and you could have caught yourselves a mess of trout. We hardly ever see anyone up here, except the members."

How much more fun we had pirating them!

I insisted on hugging the left cliff on the way out too — although the children insisted that Henry hadn't. He hadn't — he had finished with cliffs for life when he found they had only led him to the roar of the falls, instead of to the way out. But this left cliff was two miles distant from the island with the goat. I might, or might not be finished with goats — roses were easier.

So we hugged the left cliff, and that led us into Porpoise Bay, where Sechelt Inlet is separated from the Gulf of Georgia by only fifty yards of nice, soft sand. That was where Timothy, the young grey seagull, had taken Henry to show him the way out.

In the garden at home there is a little grave — with a gravestone. On it is laboriously carved, "Here lies Timothy — dead." It was supposed to say "dead of a broken wing," but there wasn't room, and the stone had been very hard. We had found him in the garden one day — very bright eyes looking at us out of a clump of long grass. He had a broken wing, which someone had evidently tried to fix with a couple of matches and a piece of fishing twine. We tried to fix it again, but he always pecked it off. We called him Timothy, because his toes were pink. But he wouldn't eat, and after a week — though surrounded by much love — he died. So they had a sorrowful funeral for him — and Peter carved his stone. That was last fall — and Timothy had just naturally wandered into the story of Henry.

Porpoise Bay was very shallow as you got in farther, and the weeds tickled the bottom of the boat, just as they had tickled Henry's tummy. It was too shallow at that stage of the tide to get into the float; but the children landed and raced across the fifty yards of nice soft sand, to look at the Gulf of Georgia.

I sat in the boat, looking at the nice soft sand. That was where Timothy had stood, his broken wing trailing, looking over his shoulder in a bewildered kind of way, asking, "Henry aren't you coming too?"

"Poor Timothy," said John, in his very saddest voice, as he climbed on board. "It was quite a long way, with a broken wing."

"I carved that gravestone, you know, John," said Peter.

"I know," said John, "but he wasn't *only* yours."

"Most of it was just a story," said Jan, firmly, as she sat down astride the bow. "And Mummy wrote it."

"I know," said Peter. "But we all helped; I said 'Contact,' you remember."

"And I said 'Sparks,'" reminded John.

Bumping heads together may be a good way to produce unusual characters — but not if you ever want to get rid of them again.

The Gathering In

OU JUST SAID SUDDENLY, "WE'LL PROBABLY LEAVE FOR home tomorrow." You started off . . . and you arrived. It wasn't really quite as simple as that. You probably decided suddenly because the weather was unexpectedly good for the moment and the glass had steadied. Calm, fine weather the last week in September is like a gift — something to be thankful for, but not expected. Nor do you refuse it, for it mightn't be offered again.

Even if you had decided, the weather never definitely decided what it was going to do until ten or eleven the next morning. Once it had committed itself, it didn't often change.

But there was always the gulf between us and home. The

156

weather on the home side of the gulf could be quite different from the side we were on. So in spite of it being fine and calm on the mainland side, we would take the binoculars and look across to beyond Texada Island. If you could see a long dark line on the sea extending south — then you knew that it was blowing hard from the west, the whole way down from Johnstone Strait. With our little boat, it would be foolish even to think of starting.

It is a good twelve hours' run from Secret Cove near Welcome Pass to home. With a favourable tide we have sometimes made it in a day. But usually, we got about two-thirds of the way there and then had to hole up for the night. By the end of September in this latitude it is almost dark by six o'clock.

Once more in sheltered waters, we could start off for the last third of the trip at any time in the morning we liked. But no one had any desire to linger — home was only forty miles away. We, who had not given Little House a thought all summer, were now straining every nerve to complete the journey far faster than our boat could run.

We had come up through these waters at the beginning of June when everything was a fresh pulsing green. The small islets and points had been covered with grass and stone crop, pink sea-thrift and small blue flowers. Everything was going somewhere ... towards some fulfilment, and was shouting out all about it. Now, in the last week in September, the hills and points were dry and brown. Green leaves were on the trees, some with a touch of yellow or a shade of pink, but they were stiff and dry and quiet. There was a stillness about everything ... it was all spent and finished with — nothing, now, had anything to say at all.

We rushed along past them — straining for our known end. The rocky points, which like prehistoric beasts had thrust out menacing jaws to stop us on our way north, now shrank back before our urgency to let us pass.

Then somebody said, "Do you remember?" and the memories poured forth, one on top of the other . . . . The hummingbird that built her nest in the rosebush just outside the window, and hatched out the black-skinned babies. The quail whose mate had been snatched up by a hawk, and who went round all spring calling, "Oh, Richard! Oh, Richard!" and Richard never answered at all. The frogs in the pond that stop singing the moment they hear a footstep, even twenty feet away, and make perfect watchdogs — but are very frustrating because you can never get near them. We never thought of Little House all summer — and now we were remembering . . . .

As we made our way down the coast into home water, the maples and alders stretched like daubs of golden paint up the dry mountain sides. The grey unconcerned cliffs stood rigid as usual, letting all the changing ideas of nature sweep around and past them. Where the point gave out the evergreens climbed past and on, sturdily up the ravines and finally there was nothing left but the granite cliffs.

There was the awful cliff with the sheer drop, where the Indian Princess was rumoured to have thrown herself over. As usual the youngsters argued about the exact spot she had chosen. The three little girls each had their favourite site and wasted no further opinions.

Peter contented himself with saying, "Wasn't she silly?" And John put his thumb in his mouth.

Now into view came the interlacing Cowichan hills — mountains really but at the moment they were only something to serve as markers of distance as we raced on at full throttle against the tide towards the "gathering in."

Four months of each summer were spent in our small boat up the long and indented coast of British Columbia, but the focal point of our lives was Little House in the middle of the forest. The central point or focus in Little House was the big stone fireplace in the corner of the living room — and the word hearth and focus both have the same meaning — the place of the fire.

Each fall when the days got shorter and the nights got colder and the maple lit their warning signals, Little House reached out, gathering us in. We could feel her gently tugging at us across the gulf and up the far coast. As long as the sun shone and the weather pattern was tranquil we turned a deaf ear and closed our minds. But a time always came when the big south-easter kept us tied to a sheltered bay — or worse when it wasn't sheltered and you spent a couple of miserable nights up every hour checking your bearings. The morning would show the whole gulf a sullen mass of great heaving waves with billowy white crests.

Following a usual pattern, the wind, when it had exhausted

itself blowing from the south-east would storm around to the west, pushing and struggling against the south-east swell it had created. By that time we would all be straining toward Little House. But there was nothing we could do but wait until the gulf was quiet, then take our chance and get across.

Then there was the last home stretch with the islands opening out one by one to let us pass. Our Gordon Setter was standing up in the dinghy now, her tail wagging. We didn't know what she was recognizing, but she knew we were home. The tide was still too low to land our equipment so we anchored off Little Cove on the south and rowed ashore. The arbutus trees that had been in bloom when we left in June were now ablaze with bright red berries. How tall the forest was, and still! The path was covered with crisp dry arbutus leaves that fell in June and our feet scrunched them as we trod over them through the trees. There stood Little House. The great maple behind glowing yellow and orange like a halo over her head.

Little House

 REMEMBER WHEN WE FIRST FOUND LITTLE HOUSE, lying all by itself in the middle of the forest. It was June-time. Everything was covered with the roses in bloom — on the paths — in the porch — over the house — up the roof . . . roses were everywhere. They formed a cordon round the house — we couldn't get near it. They caught at our legs and tugged at our clothes. "It's ours, it's ours!" they cried, and did their best to keep us out.

It was the first time we had ever found a little fairy tale house in the middle of a forest, and we didn't know quite what to do. So we called out, "Little House, Little House, who lives in Little House?" and nobody answered.

So we called louder, "Little House, Little House, who lives in Little House?" And still nobody answered.

"Well, then," we said, "we'll live here ourselves," and we crept in through the window and settled ourselves in Little House.

That was the tale the children used to tell on winter evenings, in front of the roaring fire in the big stone fireplace, about how we came to live in Little House. Just when everybody was feeling happy and contented about it, Peter always broke the peace by saying, "You're not in this, John, you weren't here at all." And John always said, "Well, I came along suddenly, and when you all answered, I said 'I'm Mr. Bear-squash-you-all-flat,' and I squashed you all flat as anything."

You would understand all this better if you had read our favourite book of the moment, *Russian Picture Tales*. In one of the stories, a mouse finds a big earthen water jar lying in a field, and thinks what a nice house it would make to live in. So he says, "Little House, Little House, who lives in Little House?" and nobody answers. So he calls louder . . . and when still nobody answers, he says, "Well then, I shall live here myself." So he settles himself in Little House. Then a frog comes along and asks the same question, and when Mr. Mouse answers that he, Mr. Mouse, does, they decide to live together. Several other animals join them, the last being Mr. Bear-squash-you-all-flat, who comes along suddenly and spoils everything by sitting down.

Anyway, our Little House looked just like a fairy tale house. It was built of half-logs with the rough bark still on, all up on end. The casement windows, in groups of three, had leaded panes. The roof was very steep, also of bark, with a great stone chimney breaking through on one side of it and a gable window on the other. There was a porch at the front of the house, and beside the porch grew a great rose bush with a trunk as big as a man's arm. It climbed up over the steep porch roof and peeked in through the leaded-paned windows of the upper room. Then, since nobody would let it in there, it scrambled up under the wide eaves and tried to find cracks into the attic, or pry the bark off the logs on the roof — for it was a very strong rose bush and had no shame.

After we had called out and asked who lived in Little House and crawled in through the unlatched window, we lost our hearts to it. For inside was a great square living room with a big stone fireplace across one corner, and a winding staircase in another. Long groups of windows with diamond panes looked deep into the green forest that crowded close. As you shrank back — a little dismayed at such dangerous living — the low dark ceiling spread itself over you, and you at once felt all right again.

Then we tiptoed through the echoing dining room; looked into the silent kitchen; crept up the winding staircase to the bedrooms, where the wooden walls sloped steeply and made the ceilings seem on strangely intimate terms with the floor.

Anyway, there it all was — fireplace, latticed windows, winding stairs, low dark ceilings and of course roses . . . one was rather helpless against them all.

When we crawled out through the window again, there on the ground right underneath the window was a round silver dollar. We considered that a very good omen, and spent it on ice cream and salve for the thorns.

Seven acres of its own land surrounded Little House. On three sides was the sea, and on the fourth side the big forest. If you hold your right arm and hand, palm up and slightly cupping the hand, thumb close in — you have a relief map of Seven Acres. You approached, as though along your arm, through half a mile of forest with the sea on your right. Seven Acres began just before you reached the hollow that your wrist makes with the joint of your thumb as it swings out. This hollow was called Big Cove — a sandy cove that cleft the high cliff for no apparent reason.

Little House faced south and slightly east, and a garden ran from the house to Little Cove — which was where the big cliff ended. The ball of your thumb and the thumb itself was the rugged cliff which rose two hundred feet up from the sea and sloped abruptly to your palm. The driveway skirted the inner base of the cliff or ball of your thumb, along where your Life Line and Line of Destiny run. And where your lines of Life and Destiny meet your Heart Line, there nestled Little House. And here too, Life and Heart brought Destiny to us.

Destiny rarely follows the pattern we would choose for it and the legacy of death often shapes our lives in ways we could not imagine. Death comes to everyone in their time — to some a parting, to some a release. We who are nearest go with them up the long golden stairs — up — up. A trumpet shrills — a gate clangs and we are left standing without. Then down the long stairs we retrace our steps to earth — an earth that is all numb and still — so still that one hears strange sounds — catches strange vagrant notes on one's heightened senses.

But small hands are tugging and voices are insistent.

161

"Will he ever come back from that other place?"

"Oh no, he doesn't want to come back!"

"Does he like it there?"

"Oh yes, he loves it."

"Well then, that's good." And happy laughter rings through the tall green pines and along the rocks and sandy beaches by the sea. No one grudges him his place in the sun.

A very special counsel was held in front of the big fireplace and summons were dispatched by Mrs. Bear to Miss Elizabeth, Miss Lou, Miss Jay and Mr. Peter.

"Of course I'll be there too," said Mrs. Bear.

It was the beginning of October and the evenings were to close in early. I knelt down and put a match to the fire in the big fireplace and while I waited for my fellow councilmen, I once more read the letters that had come that afternoon. They were full of underlined words. What one letter forgot the other ones said. "Impossible, impossible . . . impossible . . . not fair to the children. You're far too young to isolate yourself in that isolated place. Pack up at once. Just send a telegram." How nicely they had my life planned out.

I was still muttering and growling when Mr. Peter came in and seated himself panting on the council rug.

"Are you mad?" he asked glancing from my face to the letter.

"Grrrrr," I muttered.

Peter sniffed cheerfully. This was evidently going to be an interesting council. Miss Jay came in and seated herself beside him.

"She's mad," he whispered.

Jay dug her elbow hard into his ribs and ignored him. Little boys shouldn't be encouraged to speak of their mothers like that.

Then Miss Lizbeth took Mrs. Bear by the hand.

"It's dash as dash," said Mrs. Bear. "Where's Miss Lou?"

"She'll be here just in a minute, she's in a boat and she has to anchor it."

"In a boat?" I jumped to my feet.

"Mummy, Mummy," they all cried, "It's just in the woods."

"Oh," I said sinking back, "that kind of a boat." Even I knew how it was to anchor that kind of a boat and as for Miss Lou, another name she went by was, "Linger-Longer-Lou."

High leaped the flames of the council fire and the case was put before them . . . . Go back to town — *leave Little House!*

Tears flowed freely. The only thing I was able to gather at all was that everybody thought as I did. It would be impossible to leave Little House. Then when things dried up a bit we discovered that John was missing. Though he was only two and a half, John never allowed anyone to see him crying. If tears must come, and they quite often did, he shed them in private, under the stairs, in the cupboard, in Pam's kennel. No one was under the stairs. No one in the cupboard. I opened the back door. Pamela was half in, half out of her kennel and looked at me reproachfully with her liquid eyes. "What have you been doing to your offspring?" they enquired, and looked anxiously into the kennel.

"John," I called kneeling down.

"I'm not going to that old city," said a tearful voice. John who had never been to a city. "I'm going to live here with Pam."

I sent the telegram off the next day. It wasn't very polite — and I didn't care much. "Can't I?" — and did.

Seven Acres

FTER A BIG STORM WE ALWAYS HAD EXPEDITIONS AND explorings to find out how many trees had blown down and what had been cast up on the beaches — the choice depending on how strong the wind had been.

If we were going to the forest we would start off in pairs in different directions, our boundaries being fixed by mysterious points such as the Big Cedar, High Mound, Upper Water Hole, Mink Run and others that the children knew. Armed with bows and arrows and stout sticks and packages of sandwiches in our pockets we would separate. Two would go along the north sea trail, two up the back trail and John and I up the central trail — all to meet at the outer gate before the sun went down. It never worked out quite that way. How could anyone wait until the sun went down to report on an important find? Also after the sun went down one's feet turned instinctively toward Little House —

shadows might be anything. All during the expeditions explorers would crash through the forest demanding that we detour to inspect this or that find. After we had finished sorrowing over the death of a tree that Christopher Columbus might have known we would hastily compute how long the bark would last us for burning — if it were a Douglas Fir. Then we would all take mental notes of where the tree lay so that we could find it again, and off we would go our separate ways once more.

Once John and I made the biggest discovery, and the most exciting. A huge fir was down right across the road. So John and I shouted and hullooed until the other two parties broke through the forest. The big trunk had to be measured — about four feet in diameter we agreed. Then we stared blankly at each other realizing that it was also four feet of barricade and that we couldn't get our car out until the tree was sawn up. Exploring forgotten, we had to make our way down to the nearest farm and tell the farmer about our trouble. He was full of his own troubles. After we had exchanged troubles, we agreed that ours was the most pressing and that he would come out in the morning with the big saw and the sledge and wedge and we would saw our way out.

The farmer's wife had made us hot tea as the day was cold and snow lay on the ground. When we went outside again, the sun was long since down. I thought uneasily how dark it would be in the forest. The farmer perceived this and lent us a little lantern. The glass was smoked up and the wick needed trimming and it made fearsome shadows all its own. We went up the long lane from the farm, hurried up the hill and then holding hands we took long breaths and entered the forest.

How still a forest usually is! But after a big storm it is also uneasy and passed its uneasiness on to us. Uprooted trees after all are still alive and they are not used to this new position. Now and then a protesting branch would liberate itself with a sharp crack. Something snuffled and there was the sound of claws scratching on bark. A coon probably. But the heart thuds and the children crowd close to one's heels. We have to go in single file finally and Elizabeth holds the lantern higher and two shiny eyes gaze at us. We let out sighs as it bounds off.

"Deers are nothing," says Peter stoutly, holding on to my coat tails.

164

Then down the canyon hill, Big Cove lies quietly on our right; up canyon hill and now we can see sky and stars over our heads as we enter the clearing. There is the dark outline of Little House. A few more steps and the explorers break into a run. We cut around to the back door and push into a warm kitchen and oh, the blessed sound of a closed door.

It is November today and I found a little lizard, brown and orange below, standing on the cold cement floor. I stooped down to look at him. If it had been warm he would have disappeared in a flash. He was sluggish and also cold. You could feel the ton weight that held each foot from moving.

There were a dozen or more quails out in the sand pile scratching up the pale succulent roots that sand piles seem to produce. Now the quail began to jerk nervously. That means they are about to make the perilous run past the window to the flower bed. Their feet all twinkle together as they fly past and duck for shelter under the worn out weeds and naked shrubs. Then they begin to scratch and dig again, their little topknots bobbing and bobbing and bobbing. I wonder if it has uses as antenna. They are so quick to sense and transmit the slightest sound. Whizzzzz and in a burst of wing they are gone. I wish I were an artist — such simple vigorous lines would draw them. Two sharp parallel white lines on the back where the wings cling close to the body. Then more sharp white strokes at an acute angle outlining the primary feathers. The strange little black velvet mark edged with white held on with white strings over the ears. Then the scalp-lock gathered up and surmounted with a bobbing topknot.

I surprised them late the other afternoon. I cut across the path by the cedars where there is an eight-foot pole that supported a great round clump of ivy. They flew up from under my feet as I reached the cedars but instead of flying off out of sight they flew up, and dropped feet first into the bush. I clapped my hands and sure enough the ivy exploded quail in all directions.

Today a hawk chased a little quail bang up against the kitchen window. Then she sat on the window sill and shrieked. I went over to look at her but she yelled at me and said she had had all she could stand at the moment and flew off, still shrieking.

Yesterday I thought the snow was over and I swung the axe

with a reckless flourish that buried it deep in the chopping stump — and then with an equally reckless glance at the chimney, I made for the woods.

The afternoon is short in the winter and I wandered through the trees enjoying and drinking in their beauty. Every branch was laden and the slightest touch brought a silvery shower down on me. I strode through salal, each leaf piled to capacity. What matter if my boots were full of feathery loveliness? Hadn't the cold weather broken and wasn't it good to be alive? How cold the arbutus trees looked, standing sullen in their nakedness.

Back at the house I piled the fireplace with wood. That night secure in my faith that the need to stoke all night had passed, I climbed into bed with never a thought for the axe I had left in the chopping block.

Somewhere in the middle of those hours when the physical body is at its lowest ebb, I woke up. Out in the Straits fog horns wailed like lost souls. I crept out of bed and donned dressing gown and slippers and went downstairs to an almost dead fire. The clock in the flickering light showed half past two and I piled on my last remaining wood and slipped back to bed.

At half past seven I awoke again. Fog horns still moaned out in the Straits and a blinding snow drove in from the north. My breath rose like cumuli in the still room and I burrowed miserably remembering my empty wood pile and axe on the block.

Then outside my window, on a snow covered branch under the eaves a sparrow who had probably felt reckless too sang, "Why fret, why fret? Spring's coming yet."

The frogs are fairly shouting in our pond today. It has been a very late spring with some of our coldest weather after the fifteenth of March. So I suppose this business of getting the next generation under way has been somewhat delayed. A month ago I heard a few timid notes and the next day all was quiet and ice and snow had covered the pond. A whole month lost.

So today Peter and I sat on our heels right beside the water and they paid no attention whatever to us. Double circles here and double circles there in the water and, with only a nose above, out would go their clear trebling to wherever the deep thrummers had holed up for the winter. Or had they? Of if they had, where? This

166

pond life is very new to us. Four summers ago we had a hole bulldozed out for a large reservoir. When the fall rains came it turned into a pond. Late that fall a muskrat appeared and spent the winter holed up somewhere in the banks of our virgin pool. There are no lakes or streams within five miles of us so he must have come by sea. But who told our seafaring muskrat about the new pond in the middle of the forest?

The next spring, someone must have told a frog, for two or three were trying it out. That summer the news spread and life came to our pond with a rush. A lone bullrush pushed its way up in one corner, saw its own reflection and stayed. And with whatever a growing plant brings to a pond that helps water support life, came the skating bugs that cut intricate figures on the surface of the water. The little black oval scuttler beetles that dart around half submerged and willy-nilly grab any mate, came too. Soon there was plenty of food for the polywogs that wriggled around on their burrowed tails and survival was high.

Now, this fifth spring, the pond where Peter and I sit on our heels teems with all that mysteriously arrives to create a living pool. Bullrushes are breaking water in at least half the area and last year's growth still stands waist deep, dry and crisp. The frogs, perhaps brave with numbers, are trebling in sheer abandon and no movement of ours will stop them. We see a stir of green in the dry grass at the pond's edge and I pick up a little green peeper. How cold he is. His little transparent pink fingers so frail and jointed and slender lie timidly touching my palm, while its cold stomach supports its weight. His throat pulsates and he looks very worried. It seems very fat of stomach and so we decide it is a she and perhaps that explains the unwary shouting that won't be stilled.

"What is he doing, the great god Pan, down in the reeds by the river?" I asked John.

"Splashing and paddling with hoofs of a goat and breaking the golden lilies afloat as with the dragon fly in the river," answered John cuddling down beside me in bed. "Didn't you know?" he asked.

"Oh go away," I murmured sleepily.

"No we always do," waxed John indignantly.

So there was no hope. I had to waken up. But it was very

pleasant lying in bed with a little boy, telling each other all about Pan. Down below we could hear Elizabeth busy with the kitchen fire. The sun was coming in the open window and setting the lattice alight. Soon we knew there would come the call for a swim, and we would leave to go to splash and paddle in the sea, like Pan. No one could have excuses on a sunny morning.

Yet through it all ran a thin thread of routine. Elizabeth's tawny head came in the door. Tawny head, tawny eyes. Lion's eyes we called them.

"Porridge made," she announced. "Swim you two!" The head disappeared.

John and I giggled. From the noise in the back bedrooms the rest were not treated so gently. Then shrieks of laughter and a wild rush of feet down the stairs. The front door opened and they spilled out of Little House into the early sunshine.

"Come on, come on," they called.

Except for the little fertile garden, Seven Acres was mostly trees, rocks and cliffs. If you went up the hill to the east there was a ridge and the house disappeared, all but the pointed roof. If you climbed the big cliff to the south-east and looked back, you saw nothing but treetops and sky, and you thought, "Oh, dear! What has happened to Little House?" But if you remembered to look down at your feet, then you found it again — for 'way down a thin thread of smoke was rising up through the treetops.

Most of the trees that grew on Seven Acres were Douglas firs, that went up and up — great bare trunks. But far up at the top, if you held your head back, you could see the branches sprawled against the sky. Here and there among the firs were arbutus trees. They were green all the year round, shedding their old leaves as the new leaves came. They also shed their red bark and stood there cold and naked-looking, their satin-smooth skin now the palest pinks and greens. They are versatile trees, for they also bloom in the spring, holding up what at a distance look like little bunches of lily-of-the-valley. Not content with that, the flowers become bright red berries in the autumn.

When we first lived there, the big firs and balsams grew very close to the house. So close that they could lean across and whisper to each other at night. Sometimes they would keep you awake and you would forget and say sharply, "Hush, trees, go to sleep!" At first there would be an astonished silence ... then a rush of low laughter ... and they would whisper louder than ever, until you had to put your head under the blankets.

The coast of British Columbia is what is called a sinking coast. At some time, long past, there had been a great upheaval, and then subsidence. Seven Acres did not escape. Some awful force picked it up, held it at arm's length, and then let it drop sideways in an untidy muddle. Some of it held together, and the rest of it lay here and there. You could never go out for a straight stroll — you were always climbing up something, or clambering down something, making a detour. When you wanted to get to the top of the big cliff it took you ages to get there. First you had to go along the driveway. Then cut down to the left through the little copse of wild cherry and cedar. That brought you through to a half a dozen rough stone steps that led up and round a great block of stone onto a straight path. But just as you thought this might be leading somewhere, you found yourself on a long winding serpent of stepping-stones that writhes in and out, and up and down — but always higher and higher until finally you sank down breathlessly on the very tip-top of the big cliff.

If you peered cautiously over ... you could see great blocks of rock that had broken off the cliff at some past time. You would step back from the edge and look anxiously round for signs of more cracks. There was a dry reef a little way offshore, and on it cormorants sat and spread out their wings to dry between dives. Sometimes the seagulls passing would stop and gossip for a while with the cormorants; or a seal haul his fish out on the lower ledge and enjoy it in the sun. On calm days you could lie and watch the little helldivers dive down ... down ... down in the clear green water — and follow the quick turns and kick of their little pink feet, and the line of bubbles that drifted to the surface.

The smaller cliff to the east had been left on its end by the long past upheaval. All the strata, instead of lying horizontally, ran up and down and bent into groaning curves. The rock was soft, and wind and waves had worn it away until the top of the cliff was overhanging. Sixty feet above the sea, at the very edge and nonchalantly stepping off into space, poised a stunted fir tree. Time and the weather had worried and worn it — but there it persisted, sharp and simple as a Japanese print with the sea and snowpeaked Mount Baker in the background.

Island after island lay to the east and north of us. The tides in this area have a normal rise and fall of fifteen feet, though with a high wind they pile up two or three feet higher. Twice a day, these tides came and struggled through the narrow passes, pushed past the blocking islands and up the deep bay and inlets. And twice a day they gave it up and ran exhausted back to the wide ocean.

The islands sheltered us fairly well from the cold north winds, but we were open and exposed to those from the south-east. The big winter winds from that direction would drive in from Puget Sound and Juan de Fuca Straits. Higher and higher would rise the tide and the seas. With great booming roars the waves would fling themselves against the cliffs, dashing and battering them in blind fury. The coves would be a seething mass of swirling logs smashing themselves into futile splinters and scouring the beaches out of all recognition.

Salt spray from the crests of the big waves was caught up by the wind and blown a hundred yards inland — right up to Little House itself. Branches hurtled through the air and landed with deep crashes. Nobody dared to go out of doors. In the worst gusts a whole tree would fall with a mighty thud that jarred the whole house.

Then driving rain . . . dying wind . . . and finally peace. Seven Acres, stripped of everything weak or unsound, would shake the wet from its strong sound branches; run the water off its steep rocks and cliffs, and stand steaming in the misty sunlight.

. . . Yes, yes! We all remember . . . . Hurry! Hurry!

Adventura is a popular line of books from Seal Press that celebrates the achievements and experiences of women adventurers, athletes, travelers and naturalists. Please peruse the list of books below—and discover the spirit of adventure through the female gaze.

ANOTHER WILDERNESS: *Notes from the New Outdoorswoman,* edited by Susan Fox Rogers. $16.00, 1-878067-30-3.

SOLO: *On Her Own Adventure,* edited by Susan Fox Rogers. $12.95, 1-878067-74-5.

FEMME D'ADVENTURE: *Travel Tales from Inner Montana to Outer Mongolia* by Jessica Maxwell. $14.00, 1-878067-98-2.

SEASON OF ADVENTURE: *Traveling Tales and Outdoor Journeys by Women Over 50,* edited by Jean Gould. $15.95, 1-878067-81-8.

ALL THE POWERFUL INVISIBLE THINGS: *A Sportswoman's Notebook* by Gretchen Legler. $12.95, 1-878067-69-9.

A DIFFERENT ANGLE: *Fly Fishing Stories by Women,* edited by Holly Morris. $22.95, cloth, 1-878067-63-X.

UNCOMMON WATERS: *Women Write About Fishing,* edited by Holly Morris. $14.95, 1-878067-10-9.

LEADING OUT: *Women Climbers Reaching for the Top,* edited by Rachel da Silva. $16.95, 1-878067-20-6.

WATER'S EDGE: *Women Who Push the Limits in Rowing, Kayaking and Canoeing* by Linda Lewis. $14.95, 1-878067-18-4.

Ordering Information: If you are unable to obtain a Seal Press title from a bookstore, please order from us directly. Enclose payment with your order and 16.5% of the book total for shipping and handling. Washington residents should add 8.6% sales tax. Checks, MasterCard and Visa accepted. If ordering with a credit card, don't forget to include your name as it appears on the card, the expiration date and your signature. Send to Orders Department, Seal Press, 3131 Western Avenue, Suite 410, Seattle, Washington 98121. 1-800-754-0271 orders only; (206) 283-7844 phone; (206) 285-9410 fax; sealprss@scn.org. Visit our website at www.sealpress.com.